BOOK 1

RAY ALLAN
HENRY COMPTON SCHOOL, FULHAM, LONDON

MARTIN WILLIAMS
GEORGE MITCHELL SCHOOL, LEYTON, LONDON

OXFORD
UNIVERSITY PRESS

OXFORD
UNIVERSITY PRESS

Great Clarendon Street, Oxford OX2 6DP

Oxford University Press is a department of the University of Oxford.
It furthers the University's objective of excellence in research,
scholarship, and education by publishing worldwide in

Oxford   New York

Auckland   Bangkok   Buenos Aires   Cape Town   Chennai
Dar es Salaam   Delhi   Hong Kong   Istanbul   Karachi   Kolkata
Kuala Lumpur   Madrid   Melbourne   Mexico City   Mumbai   Nairobi
São Paulo   Shanghai   Taipei   Tokyo   Toronto

Oxford is a registered trade mark of Oxford University Press
in the UK and in certain other countries

British Library Cataloguing in Publication Data

Data available

ISBN 0 19 914774 4

Typeset by TechSet Ltd. Gateshead, Tyne and Wear.
Printed in Hong Kong

ABOUT THIS BOOK

Mathswise Book 1 is the first in a series of three books spanning levels 1 – 4 of the National Curriculum in England and Wales. It is aimed at students in year 7.

It has been written to give you plenty of practice at the basic concepts in mathematics so you can build up confidence and achieve your best level in the Key Stage 3 tests at the end of year 9.

The authors have many years teaching experience at this level and all the activities and exercises in this book are built on their considerable knowledge of what students in year 7 are able to understand.

Each unit in the book starts with the **learning outcomes** of the unit so that you can see what you are expected to learn.

There is a box highlighting key mathematical words

Examples are often given to show you how to approach questions. They are in blue shaded boxes, for example:

Example 1
This line is about 4 cm long.

This icon highlights Numeracy focus pages. These pages encourage numeracy practice in other contexts.

There are regular **revision exercises** throughout the book. Make sure you can do the revision questions before you move on to the next unit.

At the end of the book there is a section called **Street Maths**. This section allows you to practise all the skills you have learnt in the book. This means you can be sure you understand the concepts before moving on to the next book in the series.

The **answers** to the exercises in the book are available in a separate book from the publishers. See the back cover for details.

Contents

1 MEASUREMENT

This unit will help you to:
→ **use a ruler**
→ **measure in centimetres**
→ **recognise pairs of numbers to 10.**

Key words

unit
length
width
centimetre
measure

MEASURING IN CENTIMETRES

You often need to measure lengths or distances.

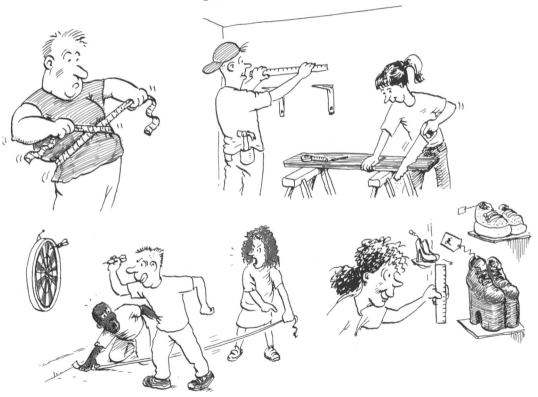

You measure short distances in **centimetres**.
A **centimetre**, cm for short, is about the width of
your little finger.

1 cm

You can use your little finger to estimate the length of a line:

Example 1
This line is about 4 cm long.

Exercise 1
Use your little finger to estimate the length of these lines:

1. ├──┤
2. ├────────────────────┤
3. ├──────┤
4. ├──────────┤
5. ├────┤
6. ├──────────────┤
7. ├────────┤
8. ├──────────────────┤
9. ├───────┤
10. ├────────────┤

You can work out the length of a line if it is marked in cm.

Example 2
This line is 3 cm long.

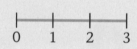

Exercise 2
These lines are marked in 1 cm sections.
Find the length of each line.

1. ├──┤
2. ├──┼──┼──┤
3. ├──┼──┼──┼──┼──┼──┼──┼──┤
4. ├──┼──┼──┼──┼──┤
5. ├──┼──┼──┼──┼──┼──┼──┤
6. ├──┼──┤
7. ├──┼──┼──┼──┤
8. ├──┼──┼──┼──┤
9. ├──┼──┼──┼──┼──┼──┼──┼──┤
10. ├──┼──┼──┼──┼──┼──┤

USING A RULER

You can use a centimetre ruler to measure lengths.

You measure from the zero mark.

Example 3

This line is 3 cm long.

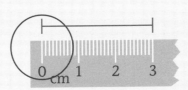

Exercise 3

Find the length of each line.

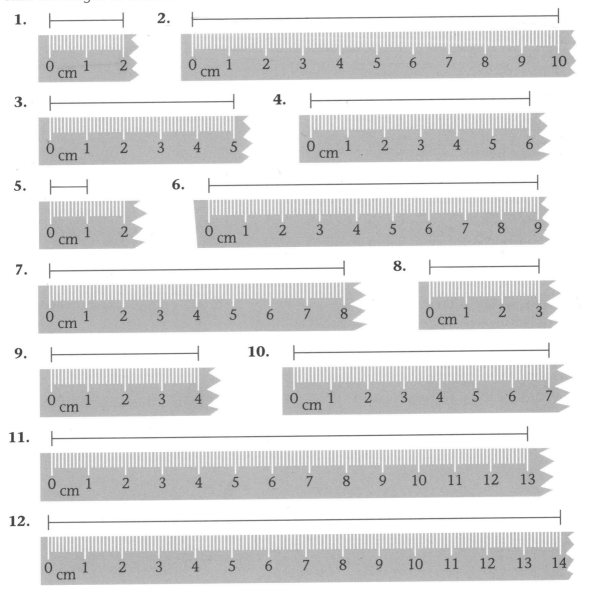

Exercise 4

Measure these lines using a centimetre ruler.

1. |————————————|

2. |——————————————————————————————|

3. |—————————————————————————|

4. |———————————————————|

5. |————————————————————|

6. |——————————|

7. |————————————————————|

8. |—————————|

9. |——————————————————————————————————|

10. |———————————————|

11. Which is the shortest line?

12. Which is the longest line?

Exercise 5

Measure these objects in centimetres.

Remember to measure from the zero mark.

1. How long is this nail?

2. How long is this needle?

3. How long is this safety pin?

4. How long is this drinking straw?

5. How long is this screw driver?

6. How long is this leaf?

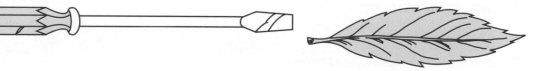

Not all lines are an exact number of centimetres.

Example 4

This ruler has half centimetre marks.

The line is $3\frac{1}{2}$ cm long.

Exercise 6

Measure these lines to the nearest half centimetre.

1. ├──────────┤ **2.** ├────────────────────────────┤

3. ├─────────────┤ **4.** ├──────────────────────┤

5. ├───┤ **6.** ├──────────────────────┤

7. ├───────────────┤ **8.** ├────────────┤

9. ├──────────────────┤ **10.** ├──────┤

11. ├──────────────────────┤ **12.** ├─┤

13. ├────────────────────────┤

14. ├─────────────────────────┤

15. ├──────────────────────────────┤

Exercise 7

Copy and complete these sentences.

1. Line D is ____ cm long.

2. Line H is ____ cm long.

3. Line ____ is $5\frac{1}{2}$ cm long.

4. Line ____ and line ____ are both the same length.

5. Line C is ____ cm long.

6. Line ____ is 5 cm long.

7. Line B is ____ cm long.

8. Line ____ is the longest line.

9. Line G is ____ cm long.

10. The shortest line is ____ cm long

A B C D E F G H

Exercise 8

Measure each object.
Copy and complete the sentence.

1. This pencil is ——— cm long.

2. This key is ——— cm long.

3. This match is ——— cm long.

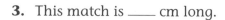

5. This bar of chocolate is ——— cm long and ——— cm wide.

4. This ink bottle is ——— cm wide and ——— cm high.

7. This ice cream is ——— cm high

6. This c omb is ——— cm long.

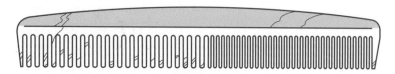

8. This penknife is ——— cm long.

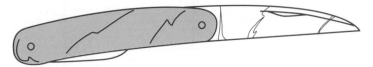

10. This lipstick is ——— cm long.

9. This screw is ——— cm long.

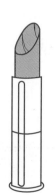

Drawing Lines

To draw a line you should

1. Put a mark at zero.
2. Use your pencil to draw the line.

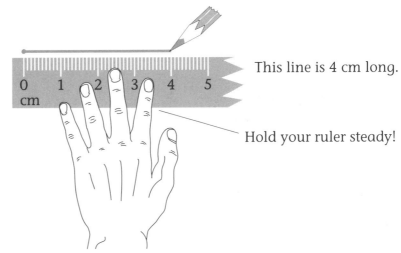

This line is 4 cm long.

Hold your ruler steady!

Exercise 9

Draw these lines.

1. 6 cm
2. 8 cm
3. 10 cm
4. 9 cm
5. 4 cm
6. 2 cm
7. 1 cm
8. 7 cm
9. 5 cm
10. 3 cm
11. $7\frac{1}{2}$ cm
12. $4\frac{1}{2}$ cm
13. $2\frac{1}{2}$ cm
14. $8\frac{1}{2}$ cm
15. $1\frac{1}{2}$ cm

You can draw lines without a ruler if you use centimetre squared paper.

Exercise 10

Draw these 'L' shapes on cm squared paper.

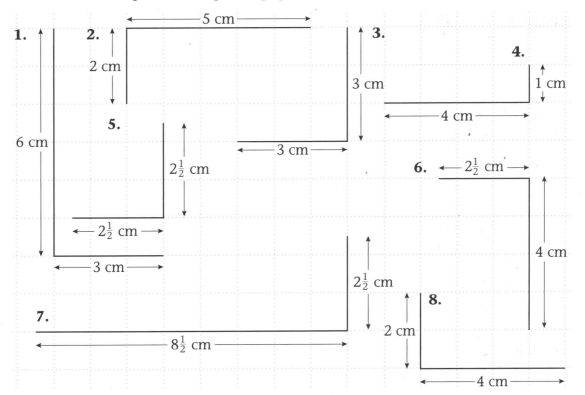

Exercise 11

Draw these shapes on cm squared paper.

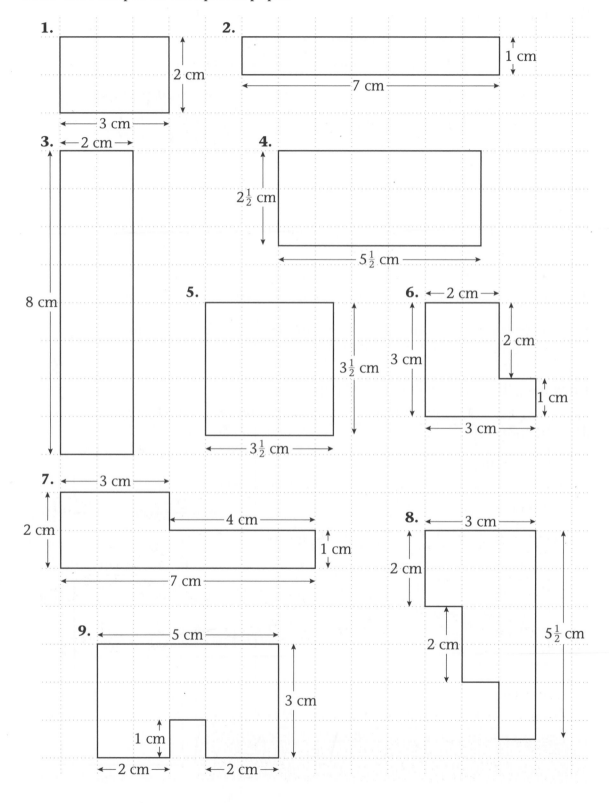

1. 2 cm, 3 cm

2. 1 cm, 7 cm

3. 2 cm, 8 cm

4. $2\frac{1}{2}$ cm, $5\frac{1}{2}$ cm

5. $3\frac{1}{2}$ cm, $3\frac{1}{2}$ cm

6. 2 cm, 2 cm, 3 cm, 1 cm, 3 cm

7. 3 cm, 4 cm, 2 cm, 1 cm, 7 cm

8. 3 cm, 2 cm, 2 cm, $5\frac{1}{2}$ cm

9. 5 cm, 3 cm, 1 cm, 2 cm, 2 cm

NUM ERACY   PAIRS TO 10

The straw is 10 cm long. It has been cut into two parts: 3 cm and 7 cm

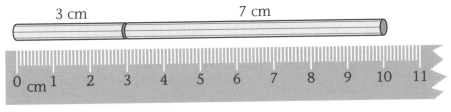

3 cm + 7 cm = 10 cm

Exercise 12

A 10 cm straw is cut into two pieces. The length of the first piece is given.
What is the length of the second piece?

1. 2 cm and ___ cm

2. 6 cm and ___ cm

3. 7 cm and ___ cm

4. 8 cm and ___ cm

5. 4 cm and ___ cm

6. 1 cm and ___ cm

7. Can you think of another cut that is not listed here?

Exercise 13

These are pieces of 10 cm straws. They have been cut and mixed up.
Measure the pieces and put them in pairs like this: A   *and*   E
                                                        3 cm   *and*   7 cm

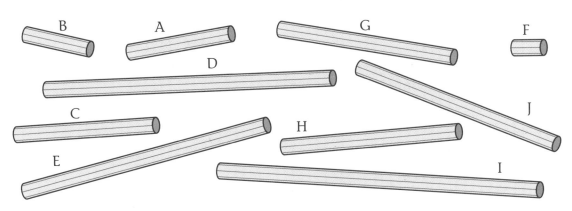

Exercise 14

There are three things wrong with this ruler. What are they?

NUMERACY MAKING CURVES FROM STRAIGHT LINES

This is a pattern made from straight lines:

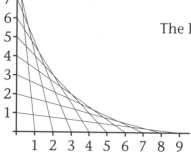

Each line joins two points.
If you add the two points you get 10.
$9 + 1 = 10$, $8 + 2 = 10$, …$1 + 9 = 10$.

The line number for this pattern is 10.

Exercise 15

1. Find the line number for each pattern.

   a 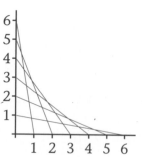   **b**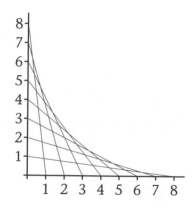

2. **a** Copy and complete this pattern.
   Use centimetre squared paper.

   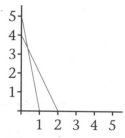

   b What is the line number for this pattern?

3. Draw a pattern with a line number
   a 8   **b** 11   **c** 12

4. Find all the pairs of numbers that add up to 20.

2 PLACE VALUE

This unit will help you to:
→ **recognise numbers up to 1000**
→ **write numbers using digits and words**
→ **understand place value**
→ **add and subtract numbers up to 100.**

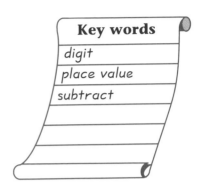

Key words

digit

place value

subtract

NUMBERS UP TO 10

All our numbers are made using the digits

0	1	2	3	4	5	6	7	8	9	*digits*
zero	one	two	three	four	five	six	seven	eight	nine	*words*

You can use an abacus to count items.

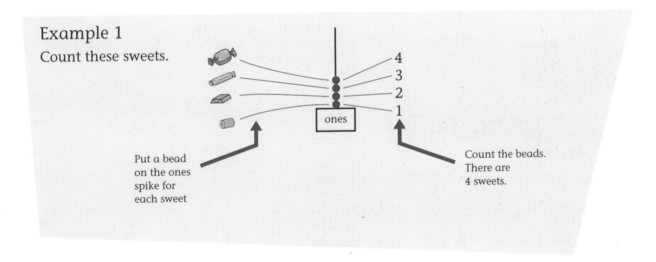

Example 1
Count these sweets.

4
3
2
1

ones

Put a bead on the ones spike for each sweet

Count the beads. There are 4 sweets.

Exercise 1
Count these items.

1.

2.

3.

4.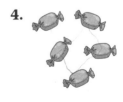

MORE THAN 9

2 digit numbers need **2** spikes.

You write numbers bigger than 9 like this:

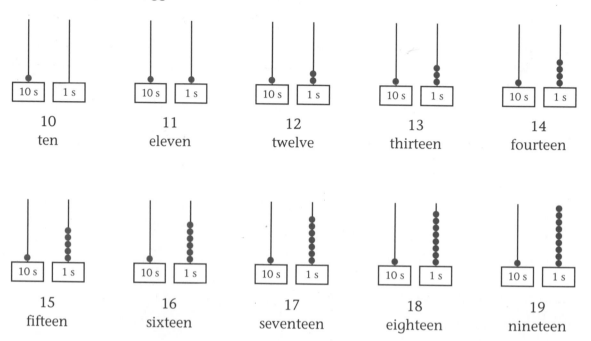

Exercise 2

Write down the number shown on each abacus.

Give your answers using digits and words.

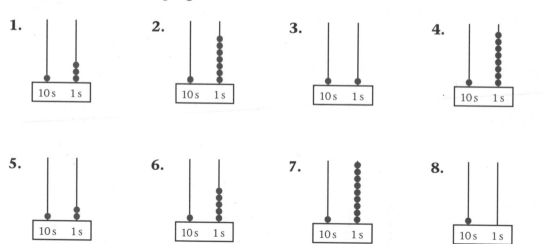

NUMBERS UP TO 100

You need to know how to write these numbers in words:

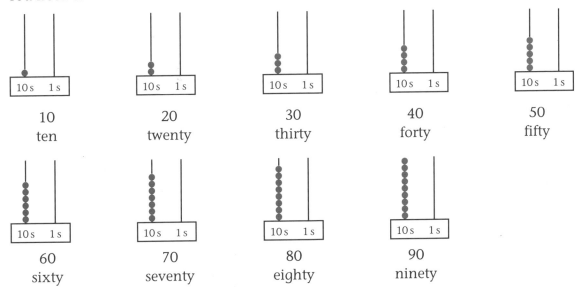

| 10 | 20 | 30 | 40 | 50 |
| ten | twenty | thirty | forty | fifty |

| 60 | 70 | 80 | 90 |
| sixty | seventy | eighty | ninety |

You can write numbers like 46 in words like this.

Imagine the abacus:

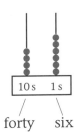

46 is forty-six   forty   six

Exercise 3

Write the number shown on each abacus in digits and in words.

1. 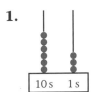   **2.**   **3.**   **4.**

5.   **6.**   **7.**   **8.**

MORE THAN 100

For three digit numbers you need three spikes:

This abacus shows 100
or one hundred

Example 2

Write down the number shown on the abacus in digits and words.

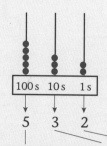

Five hundred and thirty-two

The number is 532 or five hundred and thirty-two.

Exercise 4

Write down the number shown on each abacus in digits and in words.

1.   **2.** 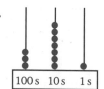   **3.**   **4.**

5. 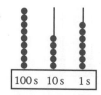   **6.**   **7.** 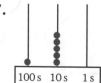   **8.**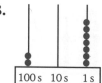

USING COUNTERS

You can show numbers using counters.

Example 3

100 s	10 s	1 s

These counters show: 3   2   5

3 hundred and twenty-five

Exercise 5

Write down the total shown by the counters.

Give your answers in digits and words.

1.
100 s	10 s	1 s

2.
100 s	10 s	1 s

3.
100 s	10 s	1 s

4.
100 s	10 s	1 s

5.
100 s	10 s	1 s

6.
100 s	10 s	1 s

7.
100 s	10 s	1 s

8.
100 s	10 s	1 s

9.
100 s	10 s	1 s

10.
100 s	10 s	1 s

11.
100 s	10 s	1 s

12.
100 s	10 s	1 s

13.
100 s	10 s	1 s

14.
100 s	10 s	1 s

15.
100 s	10 s	1 s

Exercise 6

Draw boxes of your own. Fill in the boxes to show these numbers.

1. 425

2. 333

3. 214

4. 28

5. 320

6. 909

ADDING AND SUBTRACTING UNITS USING AN ABACUS

You can use an abacus to add numbers.

Example 4

Add 4 to this abacus.
Copy and complete:

13 + 4 = ☐

Put 4 more beads on
the one spike:

13 + 4 = 17

Exercise 7

Copy and complete the sentences.

1. Add 6 to this:

21 + 6 = ☐

2. Add 3 to this:

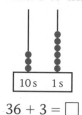

36 + 3 = ☐

3. Add 9 to this:

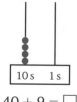

40 + 9 = ☐

4. Add 7 to this:

52 + 7 = ☐

5. Add 2 to this:

65 + 2 = ☐

6. Add 5 to this:

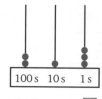

213 + 5 = ☐

Exercise 8

Copy and complete the sentences.

The first one has been done for you.

1. Take 4 away:

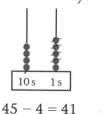

45 − 4 = 41

2. Take 6 away:

58 − 6 = ☐

3. Take 3 away:

35 − 3 = ☐

ADDING TENS

You can add tens in your head if you think about an abacus.

Example 5
Find 25 + 20

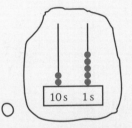

Imagine 25 on an abacus

To add 20 you add 2 tens

So 25 + 20 = 45.

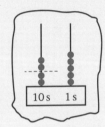

Exercise 9

Copy and complete the sentences.

1. Add 30 to this:

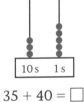

13 + 30 = ☐

2. Add 20 to this:

42 + 20 = ☐

3. Add 40 to this:

35 + 40 = ☐

4.

16 + 60 = ☐

5.

1 + 50 = ☐

6.

70 + 10 = ☐

7. 36 + 10 = ☐

8. 42 + 20 = ☐

9. 38 + 40 = ☐

10. 52 + 30 = ☐

11. 12 + 40 = ☐

12. 19 + 50 = ☐

13. 38 + 60 = ☐

14. 28 + 50 = ☐

15. 49 + 40 = ☐

SUBTRACTING TENS

You can subtract or 'take away' by taking beads off the abacus.

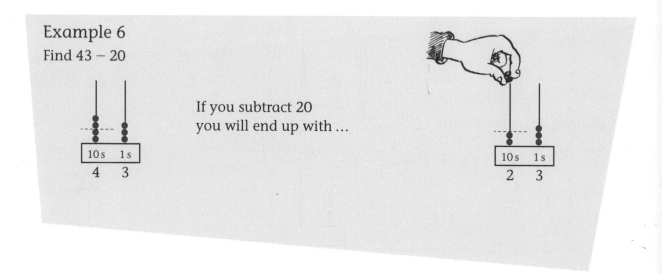

Example 6

Find 43 − 20

If you subtract 20
you will end up with …

Exercise 10

Work these out in your head. Use the pictures of the abacus to help you.

a   Take 20 from each number.

b   Subtract 30 from each number.

c   You can subtract 50 from only some of the numbers below. Find those numbers
and take away 50.

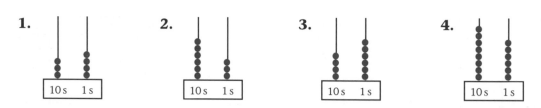

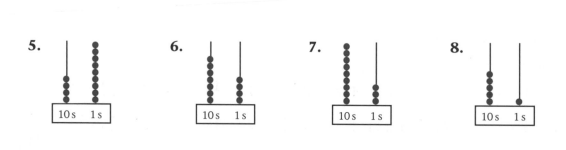

Mᴏʀᴇ ᴀᴅᴅɪɴɢ

Example 7

Use counters to work out 23 + 44

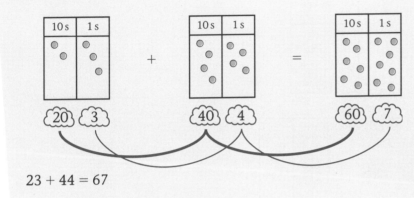

23 + 44 = 67

Exercise 11

For each addition

a   draw the answer box

b   write the addition 'sentence' in digits.

1. [10s | 1s] + [10s | 1s]

2. [10s | 1s] + [10s | 1s]

3. [10s | 1s] + [10s | 1s]

4. [10s | 1s] + [10s | 1s]

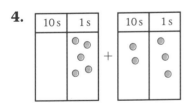

5. [10s | 1s] + [10s | 1s]

6. [10s | 1s] + [10s | 1s]

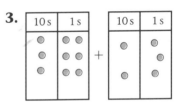

Exercise 12

Work out these additions.

Use counters or an abacus to help you.

1. ☐ + 12 = 17

2. 42 + ☐ = 49

3. ☐ + 13 = 17

4. 27 + ☐ = 39

5. ☐ + 81 = 87

6. ☐ + 32 = 39

7. ☐ + 2 = 9

8. 51 + ☐ = 58

MORE SUBTRACTING

Example 8

Work out $63 - 21$.

Using counters, start with 63:

10s	1s

Take away 2 tens and a 1 to leave

10s	1s

42

So $63 - 21 = 42$

Exercise 13

Copy and complete these sentences.

1. Take 23 from:

10s	1s

$35 - 23 = \square$

2. Take 16 from:

10s	1s

$97 - 16 = \square$

3. Take 34 from:

10s	1s

$87 - 34 = \square$

4. Take 41 from:

10s	1s

$83 - 41 = \square$

5. Take 42 from:

10s	1s

$53 - 42 = \square$

6. Take 16 from:

10s	1s

$37 - 16 = \square$

7. $96 - 13 = \square$

8. $64 - 41 = \square$

9. $99 - 83 = \square$

10. $65 - 23 = \square$

11. $91 - 21 = \square$

12. $27 - 16 = \square$

13. $33 - 31 = \square$

14. $46 - 42 = \square$

15. $55 - 45 = \square$

CROSSING OVER

Remember that you can only fit
9 beads on an abacus spike:

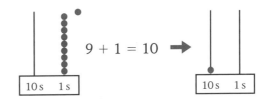

$9 + 1 = 10$

When you add another 1 the place value changes.

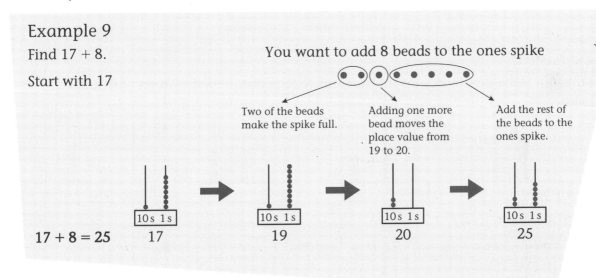

Example 9

Find $17 + 8$.

Start with 17

You want to add 8 beads to the ones spike

Two of the beads make the spike full.

Adding one more bead moves the place value from 19 to 20.

Add the rest of the beads to the ones spike.

$17 + 8 = 25$ 17   19   20   25

Exercise 14

Copy and complete the sentences:

1. Add 5:

$9 + 5 = \square$

2. Add 7:

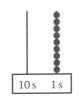

$9 + 7 = \square$

3. Add 9:

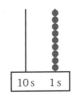

$9 + 9 = \square$

4. Add 3:

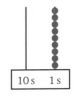

$9 + 3 = \square$

5. Add 25:

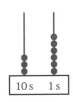

$36 + 25 = \square$

6. Add 36:

$46 + 36 = \square$

7. Add 43:

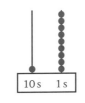

$19 + 43 = \square$

8. Add 27:

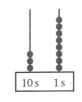

$38 + 27 = \square$

MAKING UP PROBLEMS FOR YOURSELF

Example 10

The abacus shows 35. You can make 35 in many ways, like this:

$35 = 21 + 14$ *or* $35 = 18 + 17$

$35 = 45 - 10$ *or* $35 = 42 - 7$

Exercise 15

Make up some additions and subtractions for the numbers shown on each abacus below.

1.   **2.** 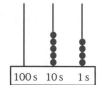 **3.**   **4.**

5.   **6.**   **7.**   **8.**

Exercise 16

Answer the questions below as quickly as you can.

1. a	$24 + 13$	**b** $32 + 16$	**c** $15 + 14$
2. a	$26 - 13$	**b** $32 - 11$	**c** $76 - 23$
3. a	$32 + 10$	**b** $56 + 14$	**c** $44 + 18$
4. a	$32 - 9$	**b** $64 - 15$	**c** $50 - 11$
5. a	$120 + 19$	**b** $152 + 116$	**c** $263 + 25$
6. a	$119 - 20$	**b** $234 - 50$	**c** $419 - 60$
7. a	$123 + 28$	**b** $238 + 36$	**c** $346 + 129$
8. a	$131 - 61$	**b** $327 - 95$	**c** $434 - 85$
9. a	$236 + 162$	**b** $356 + 285$	**c** $567 + 52$
10. a	$136 - 97$	**b** $218 - 119$	**c** $300 - 197$

③ SHAPE

This unit will help you to:
→ **recognise and name circles, squares, rectangles, kites and triangles**
→ **understand the terms radius and diameter**
→ **produce patterns with circles**
→ **find lines of symmetry.**

NAMING SHAPES

You need to know the names of these shapes:

Circle	Square	Rectangle	Kite	Triangle
One curved side	Four straight equal sides	Four straight sides	Four straight sides	Three straight sides

Exercise 1

Write the name of these shapes:

1.
2.
3.
4.
5.

6.
7.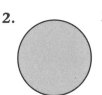
8.
9.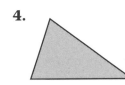
10.

Exercise 2

Write down all the shapes that you see in each drawing.

1.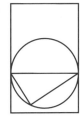
2.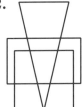
3.
4.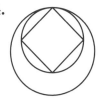
5.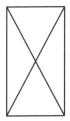

Exercise 3

Copy and complete these sentences about the picture.

1. I see 6 circles in this drawing.

2. I see _____ squares in this drawing.

3. I see _____ triangles in this drawing.

4. I see _____ rectangles in this drawing.

5. I see _____ kites in this drawing.

6. The shapes of Dozo's nose is a _____ .

7. In one hand Dozo is holding three different shapes. These are _____ , _____ and _____ .

8. The shape that Dozo's foot stands on is a _____ .

Exercise 4

Copy and complete these sentences about the picture.

1. Shape A is a _____ .

2. Shapes B and F are _____ .

3. Shape C is a _____ .

4. Shape D is a _____ .

5. Shape E is a _____ .

6. There are _____ kites in the picture.

7. There are _____ circles in the picture.

8. There are _____ rectangles in the picture.

Remember to count these shapes too.

DRAWING CIRCLES

You need a pair of compasses.

You can draw circles around the edge of a coin:

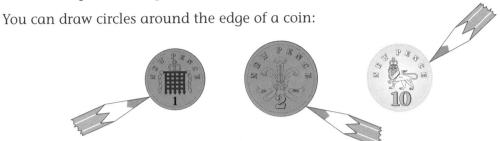

To draw a circle accurately you use a pair of compasses.

A pair of compasses has two ends:

The pointed end
stays at the centre
of the circle.

This distance
is the **radius**
of the circle.

The pencil end
draws the edge
of the circle.

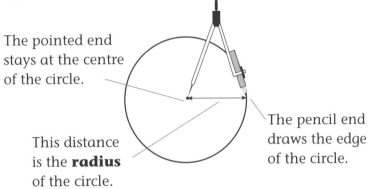

ACTIVITY SPRINGS

Look at the finished circle pattern at the bottom of the page.
Use your compass to draw the 'spring' pattern accurately

1. Draw a curved
guideline – use a
compass or draw
it freehand.
Draw the curve
lightly.

2. Set your compass to $2\frac{1}{2}$
cm. Put your compass
point at one end of the
curve and draw a circle.
Move a small distance
along the curve and
draw another circle.

3. Repeat this until you
complete the pattern and it
looks like this. The more
circles you add, the smoother
the pattern will look.

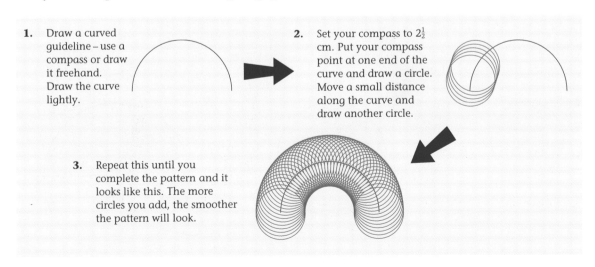

Example 1

Draw a circle with radius 3 cm.

Set the compasses so the distance is 3 cm:

Draw the circle:

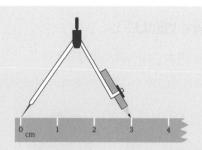

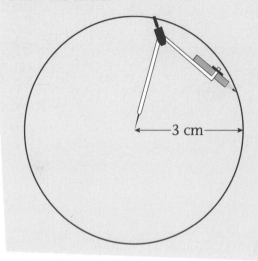

Exercise 5

Draw these circles carefully.

1. Radius 2 cm

2. Radius 4 cm

3. Radius 3 cm

4. Radius 5 cm

5. Radius 6 cm

6. Radius $2\frac{1}{2}$ cm

7. Radius $3\frac{1}{2}$ cm

8. Radius $1\frac{1}{2}$ cm

9. Radius $4\frac{1}{2}$ cm

Exercise 6

Measure the radius of each circle.

1.

2.

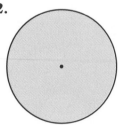

3.

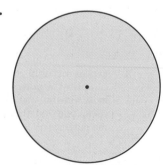

NUMERACY RADIUS AND DIAMETER

The radius
of a circle

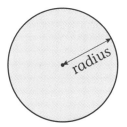

The distance from
the centre to the
edge of a circle

The diameter
of a circle

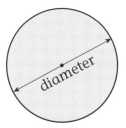

The distance across
a circle passing
through the centre

The London eye is
the largest big wheel.
Its diameter is 134m.
Its radius is 67m.

Example 2

A circle has a radius of 4 cm.
What is its diameter?

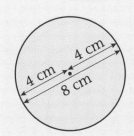

If the radius is 4 cm
the diameter is 4 cm + 4 cm = 8 cm
or 4 cm × 2 = 8 cm

Exercise 7

1. Each of these is a radius of a circle.
For each circle find the diameter.

a 2 cm	**b** 5 cm	**c** 1 cm	**d** 4 cm	**e** 6 cm
f 3 cm	**g** 10 cm	**h** 7 cm	**i** 9 cm	**j** 8 cm

2. These are the diameters of some circles.
For each circle find the radius.

a 8 cm	**b** 4 cm	**c** 10 cm	**d** 6 cm	**e** 2 cm
f 12 cm	**g** 16 cm	**h** 14 cm	**i** 20 cm	**j** 18 cm

ACTIVITY   CIRCUMFERENCE

The circumference of a circle is the distance around the edge.

About how many **times** does the diameter fit round the circumference?

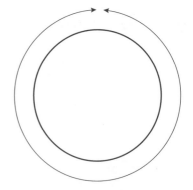

ACTIVITY   CIRCLE PATTERNS

Here is a pattern made from circles and straight lines.

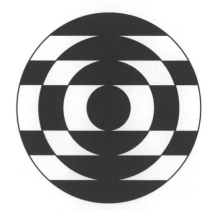

Follow these steps to make your own pattern:

1. In the middle of your page mark a centre point C.

2. With your compass point kept on the point C, draw these circles:

    a radius 1 cm   **b** radius 2 cm

    c radius 3 cm   **d** radius 4 cm

    (These are called concentric circles. They have the same centre.)

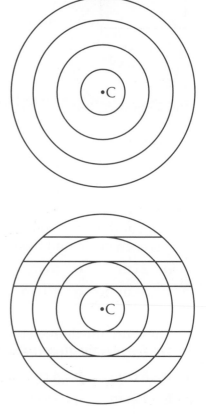

3. Draw straight lines across the largest circle. The lines must be the same distance apart at both ends. Draw the lines so that they just touch the edges of the smaller circle.

4. Think of your own colour scheme to decorate your pattern.

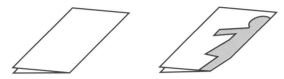

Activity Line symmetry

Fold a piece of paper … then draw a shape and cut it out.

Unfold the shape. You will have a **symmetrical shape**. Both halves will be exactly the same.

The crease down the middle of the shape is called the **line of symmetry**.

Here are some examples. Try to make some of your own.

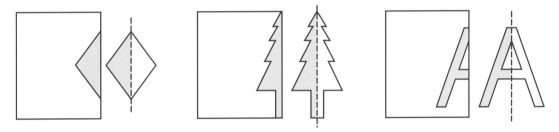

Exercise 8
Find the other half of the monster's face so that his face is symmetrical.

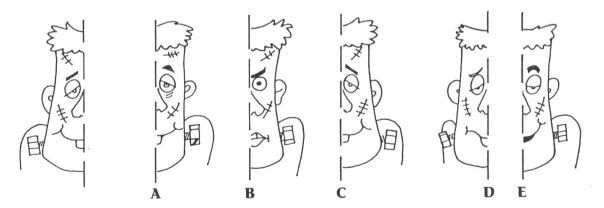

A   B   C   D   E

Be careful. All the faces look similar.

If you want to see the monster's face, place a mirror along the broken line of symmetry.

Exercise 9

Complete the pictures so they are **symmetrical**.

For example:

1.

2.

3.

4.

5.

6.

7.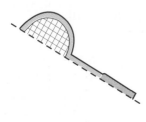

8.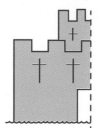

9.

10.

11.

12.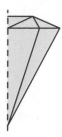

Exercise 10

These shapes have lost their partner. The partner makes the shape symmetrical.

For example:

A and Y are partners:

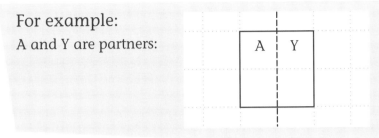

Find the partners. Write your answers like this: A and Y, B and ___, C and ___ .

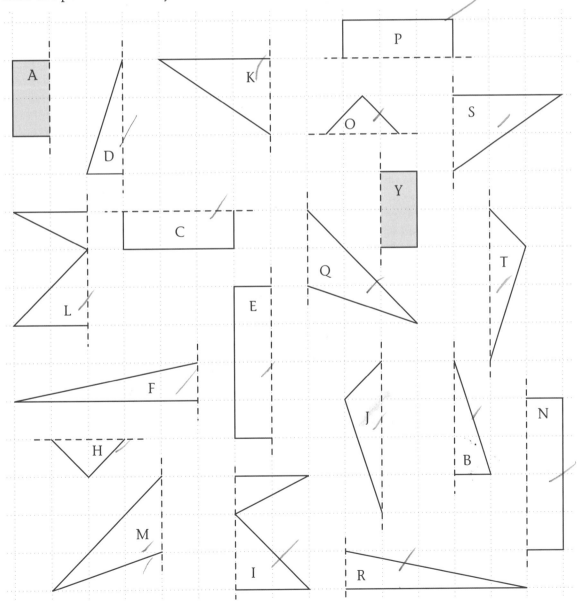

You can use your a mirror to check your line of symmetry is correct.

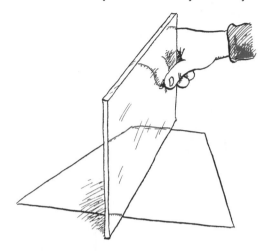

Example 3

Which pictures show lines of symmetry?
Answer YES or NO.

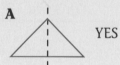 YES

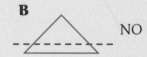 NO

Exercise 11

Which pictures show lines of symmetry?
Answer YES or NO.

1.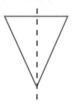

2.

3.

4.

5.

6.

7.

8.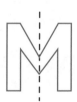

9.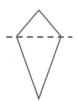

10.

11.

12.

MORE THAN ONE LINE OF SYMMETRY

Some shapes have more than one line of symmetry.

For example, this shape has two lines of symmetry.

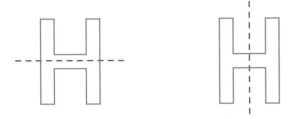

Exercise 12

1. Draw all the lines of symmetry on these shapes using dotted lines.
Check your lines with a mirror.

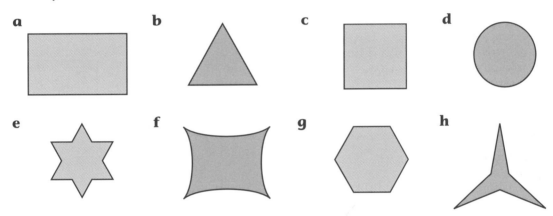

2. Some of these letters have lines of symmetry.
Draw all the lines of symmetry you can find.

ABCDEFGHIJKLM
NOPQRSTUVWXYZ

3. Look around the room.
Sketch any things that look symmetrical.
Draw in the lines of symmetry.

4 BASIC ARITHMETIC

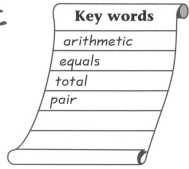

Key words

arithmetic

equals

total

pair

This unit will help you to:
→ develop mental arithmetic methods
→ add and subtract up to 100 using a number line
→ use shortcuts to add more than two numbers.

ADDITION UP TO 10

Remember: To add two sets of items together you count on.

Example 1

a Which box has the most sweets?
b How many sweets are there altogether?

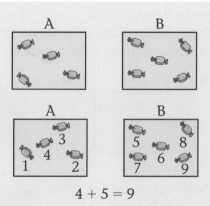

a A has 4 sweets and B has 5 sweets.
B has the most sweets
b Altogether there are 9 sweets.

$$4 + 5 = 9$$

Exercise 1

Solve these problems. See how many you can do in 10 minutes.

1. How many mushrooms altogether?

2. How many apples altogether?

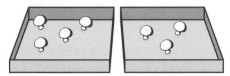

3. Which box has the most crosses?

4. Which box has the most dots?

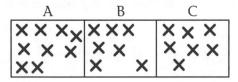

5. 2 and 5 is ___

6. 5 and 4 is ___

7. 4 plus 3 is ___

8. 2 and 7 equals ___

9. 8 and 1 equals ___

10. 6 and 2 makes ___

11. 7 and 0 is ___

12. 4 plus 5 equals ___

13. 0 and 9 makes ___

14. 2 and 5 equals ___

15. 4 plus 4 equals ___

16. 3 and 6 makes ___

ADDING IN 10S

Fatima can throw the cricket ball exactly 10 m.

If she starts at the 9 m mark the ball will land at the 19 m mark.

$9 + 10 = 19$

Exercise 2

Find where Fatima's throw will land for each of these starting points.
This number line will help you:

```
0   10   20   30   40   50   60   70   80   90   100
```

1. 6 m	**2.** 2 m	**3.** 5 m	**4.** 1 m	**5.** 7 m	**6.** 8 m
7. 12 m	**8.** 16 m	**9.** 19 m	**10.** 13 m	**11.** 17 m	**12.** 20 m
13. 30 m	**14.** 40 m	**15.** 70 m	**16.** 80 m	**17.** 82 m	**18.** 85 m

Exercise 3

Add 10 to each number as quickly as you can, in your head.

1. 19	**2.** 23	**3.** 32	**4.** 51	**5.** 58
6. 62	**7.** 36	**8.** 17	**9.** 36	**10.** 47

Exercise 4

The pattern in each set of numbers below is 'add 10'.
Find the missing numbers.

1. 21, 31, 41, ____, ____, ____, 81

2. 19, 29, ____, ____, 59, ____, ____

3. 8, 18, ____, ____, ____, ____, 68

4. 16, 26, ____, ____, ____, ____, 76

5. 12, ____, ____, ____, ____, ____, 72

ADDING 20

Example 2

Work out $12 + 20$
20 is two jumps of 10. On this number line you can add 20 by adding 2 jumps of 10.

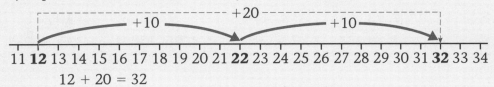

$12 + 20 = 32$

Exercise 5

Add 20 to each number. Do them in your head.

1. 20	**2.** 16	**3.** 25	**4.** 39	**5.** 62	**6.** 7
7. 51	**8.** 78	**9.** 33	**10.** 59	**11.** 71	**12.** 100

TAKING AWAY IN 10S

You can use a number line to help you take away 10:

Example 3

Work out $27 - 10$
Use the number line to jump back 10.

$$27 - 10 = 17$$

Exercise 6

Take away 10 from each number. Do them as quickly as you can in your head.

1. 40	**2.** 20	**3.** 50	**4.** 70	**5.** 19
6. 37	**7.** 21	**8.** 63	**9.** 94	**10.** 56
11. 33	**12.** 86	**13.** 77	**14.** 59	**15.** 120

TAKING AWAY 20

Example 4

Work out $41 - 20$
20 is two jumps of 10. If you want to take away 20 from a number, take away 2 jumps of 10.

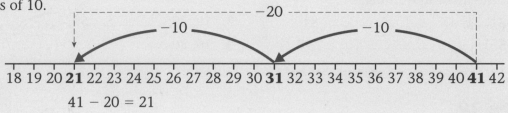

$$41 - 20 = 21$$

Exercise 7

Take 20 from each number.

1. 40	**2.** 70	**3.** 50	**4.** 25	**5.** 85
6. 23	**7.** 73	**8.** 67	**9.** 46	**10.** 71
11. 88	**12.** 39	**13.** 35	**14.** 150	**15.** 186

Exercise 8

Answer these take away problems. Do them in your head.

1. A rope is 65 m long. 20 m is cut from the rope. How many metres of rope are left?

2. A plank of wood is 97 cm long. 10 cm is cut from the plank. What length of plank is left?

3. 77 people are on a train. 20 of them get off. How many people are left on the train?

MORE THAN 10

You can use the number line to add numbers that are more than 10.

Example 5
Work out 13 + 12

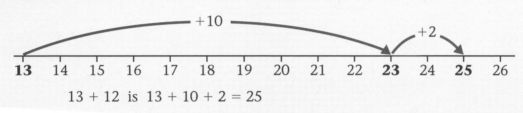

13 + 12 is 13 + 10 + 2 = 25

Exercise 9
Do these in your head; add 10, then add the rest.

1. 13 + 13   **2.** 15 + 12   **3.** 16 + 13   **4.** 14 + 11   **5.** 12 + 16

6. 13 + 16   **7.** 9 + 11   **8.** 10 + 13   **9.** 15 + 14   **10.** 21 + 15

11. 26 + 12   **12.** 31 + 14   **13.** 52 + 13   **14.** 42 + 15   **15.** 36 + 12

Example 6
Work out 8 + 23

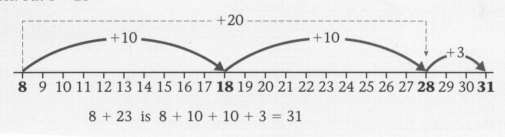

8 + 23 is 8 + 10 + 10 + 3 = 31

Exercise 10
Add these numbers.

1. 21 + 23   **2.** 30 + 26   **3.** 13 + 24   **4.** 25 + 24   **5.** 45 + 22

6. 52 + 23   **7.** 36 + 22   **8.** 41 + 26   **9.** 52 + 27   **10.** 17 + 23

11. 25 + 25   **12.** 39 + 23   **13.** 77 + 25   **14.** 56 + 25   **15.** 78 + 23

Exercise 11

1. The pairs of numbers must hit the target number: 20.
   Find what the ? stands for on each arrow line.

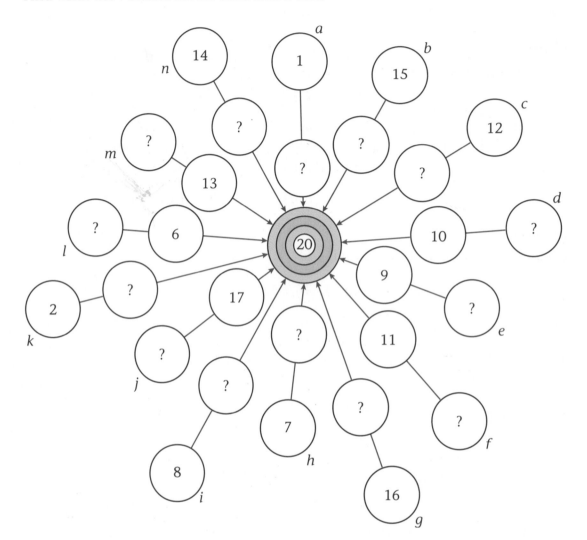

2. Find the number that goes into each of the boxes below.

   a $3 + \square = 20$ **b** $\square + 5 = 20$ **c** $10 + \square = 20$ **d** $14 + \square = 20$

   e $18 + \square = 20$ **f** $20 = \square + 17$ **g** $20 = 1 + \square$ **h** $20 = 20 + \square$

   i $11 + \square = 20$ **j** $13 + \square = 20$

Exercise 12

In the diagram in Exercise 11 find what each ? stands for if you change the target
number to:

1. 30   **2.** 50   **3.** 100

SHORTCUTS TO ADDITION

You can use shortcuts to add numbers.
Look for pairs of numbers that add up to 10 or 20.

Example 7

Work out $12 + 9 + 7 + 8 + 3 + 1 + 2 + 18 + 2$

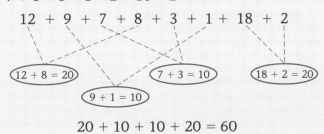

$12 + 9 + 7 + 8 + 3 + 1 + 18 + 2$

$12 + 8 = 20$ $7 + 3 = 10$ $18 + 2 = 20$

$9 + 1 = 10$

$20 + 10 + 10 + 20 = 60$

Exercise 13

Follow the example to find these totals:

1. $13 + 14 + 5 + 7 + 6 + 9 + 11 + 5 = \boxed{}$

$13 +\_\_=\_\_$ ◯   ◯   ◯

$\square + \square + \square + \square$

2. $23 + 7 + 16 + 3 + 17 + 2 + 8 + 4 = \boxed{}$

◯ +   ◯ + $3 +\_\_=\_\_$ ◯

3. $5 + 7 + 4 + 16 + 19 + 3 + 9 + 11 + 1 + 15 = \boxed{}$

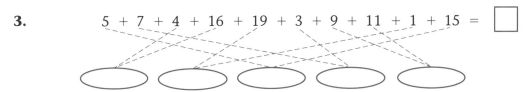

Exercise 14

Find these totals:

1. $7 + 16 + 3 + 3 + 9 + 11 + 17 + 20 = \square$

2. $4 + 14 + 7 + 13 + 5 + 5 + 15 + 6 + 15 = \square$

3. $13 + 9 + 12 + 8 + 18 + 1 + 7 + 12 + 2 = \square$

4. $14 + 16 + 4 + 9 + 15 + 11 + 6 + 10 = \square$

5. $3 + 17 + 9 + 8 + 2 + 12 + 18 + 11 = \square$

6. $20 + 15 + 11 + 18 + 1 + 5 + 19 + 9 = \square$

OTHER TOTALS

Example 8

Which two numbers from this circle add up to 12?

7 and 5 add up to 12.

Exercise 15

1.
a Which two numbers add up to 15?
b Which two numbers add up to 10?
c Which two numbers add up to 5?

2.
a Which two numbers add up to 19?
b Which two numbers add up to 14?
c Which two numbers add up to 10?

3.
a Which two numbers add up to 16?
b Which two numbers add up to 12?
c Which two numbers add up to 13?

4.
a Which two numbers add up to 20?
b Which two numbers add up to 16?
c Which two numbers add up to 12?

5.
a Which two numbers add up to 23?
b Which two numbers add up to 32?
c Which two numbers add up to 14?

6.
a Which two numbers add up to 27?
b Which two numbers add up to 18?
c Which two numbers add up to 24?

Exercise 16

Draw a circle and inside it write six numbers which can be used to add up to these totals. Do not use the totals themselves in the circle.

1. 25, 17 and 48

2. 35, 18, and 27

NUMBER SQUARES

Example 9

To complete a number square, follow these steps.

2	3	
5	1	
		☐

Add the numbers across

2	3	5
5	1	6
		☐

Now add the numbers downwards

2	3	5
5	1	6
7	4	☐

2	3	5
5	1	6
7	4	11

Now add the answers across and then down. The answer should be the same both ways

Exercise 17

Complete these number squares.

1.
3	4	
4	5	
		☐

2.
6	3	
5	5	
		☐

3.
7	2	
3	6	
		☐

4.
4	3	
6	5	
		☐

5.
6	5	
4	7	
		☐

6.
8	3	
1	8	
		☐

7.
7	5	
3	4	
		☐

8.
6	2	
6	7	
		☐

9.
8	4	
6	7	
		☐

10.
2	9	
8	4	
		☐

11.
8	5	
7	6	
		☐

12.
9	6	
5	8	
		☐

13.
8	3	
4	11	
		☐

14.
5	6	
12	5	
		☐

15.
8	6	
11	7	
		☐

16.
13	6	
4	9	
		☐

17.
14	6	
3	13	
		☐

18.
7	15	
5	5	
		☐

19.
12	12	
6	9	
		☐

20.
4	16	
8	6	
		☐

5 SORTING

This unit will help you to:
→ **sort objects into groups.**

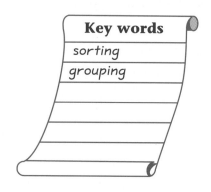

Key words

sorting

grouping

MATCHING PAIRS

Exercise 1

1. Complete this table by joining the matching pairs in the boxes.

Left box	Right box
A	J
B	K
C	L
D	M
E	N
F	O
G	P
H	Q

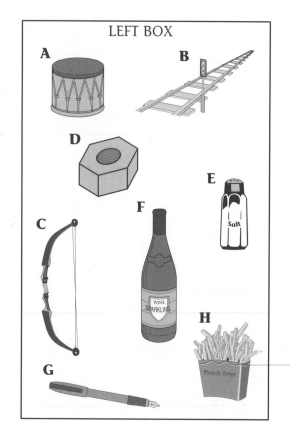

LEFT BOX

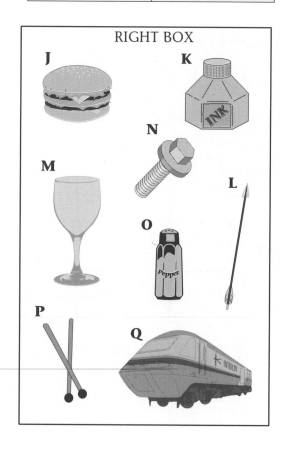

RIGHT BOX

2. Match these pairs:

salt and	queen
cats and	boys
heads and	pepper
king and	coat
left and	tails
girls and	dogs
hot and	fork
oranges and	right
hat and	lemons
knife and	cold

WHERE DOES IT GO?

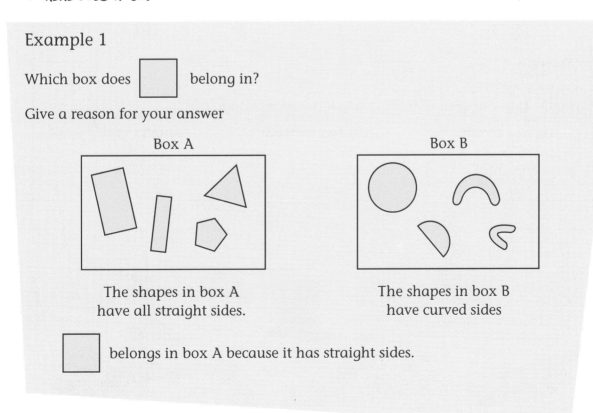

Example 1

Which box does ▢ belong in?

Give a reason for your answer

Box A

Box B

The shapes in box A
have all straight sides.

The shapes in box B
have curved sides

▢ belongs in box A because it has straight sides.

Exercise 2

For each question give a reason for your answer.

1. Which box does 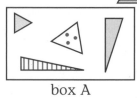 belong in?

box A   box B

2. Which box does 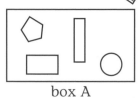 belong in?

box A   box B

3. Which box does 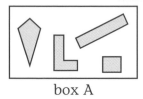 belong in?

box A   box B   box C

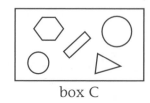

Exercise 3

Copy these rings.
Write the name of each of these items in the correct ring.

things to eat   **things to wear**   **sports equipment**

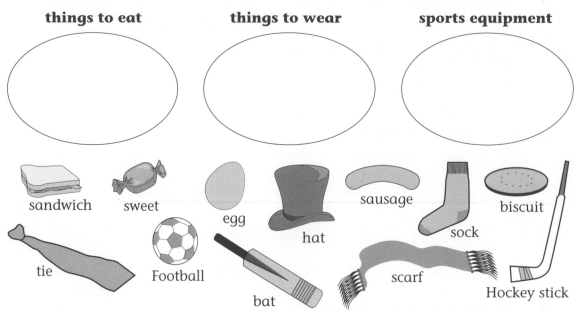

sandwich   sweet   egg   hat   sausage   sock   biscuit

tie   Football   bat   scarf   Hockey stick

Exercise 4

Sarah chooses shapes that are made from straight lines.
Ross chooses shapes made from curves.

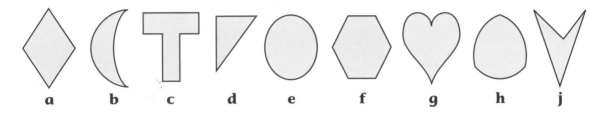

a   **b**   **c**   **d**   **e**   **f**   **g**   **h**   **j**

1. Make two lists to sort these shapes for Sarah and Ross.

   For example: Sarah   Ross

                       a   **e**

2. Where would you place this shape?
   Give a reason for your answer.

3. These words can be sorted into different lists.

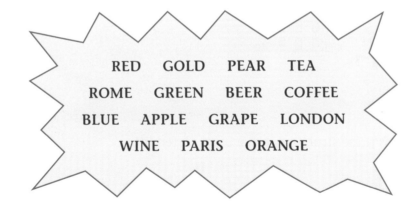

RED   GOLD   PEAR   TEA
ROME   GREEN   BEER   COFFEE
BLUE   APPLE   GRAPE   LONDON
WINE   PARIS   ORANGE

   a   Copy and complete the table:

Colours	Drinks	Cities

   b   Which word belongs in two lists?

SORTING INTO GROUPS

These structures can be sorted in different ways.

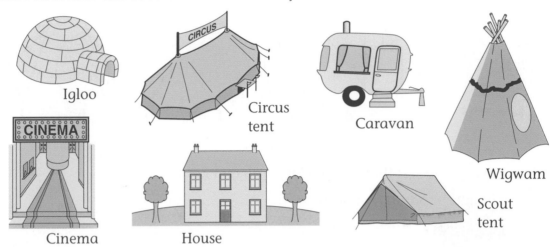

Here they have been sorted into two groups.

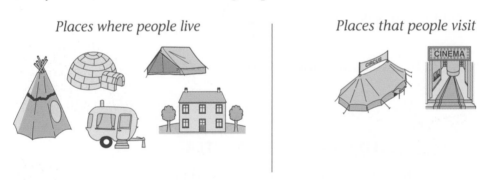

Places where people live

Places that people visit

Exercise 5

1. Say what groups these structures have been sorted into.

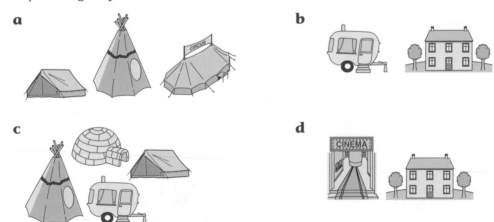

a

b

c

d

2. Find other ways these structures can be sorted.

Exercise 6

These stamps can be sorted in different ways.
List the ways that the stamps can be sorted.

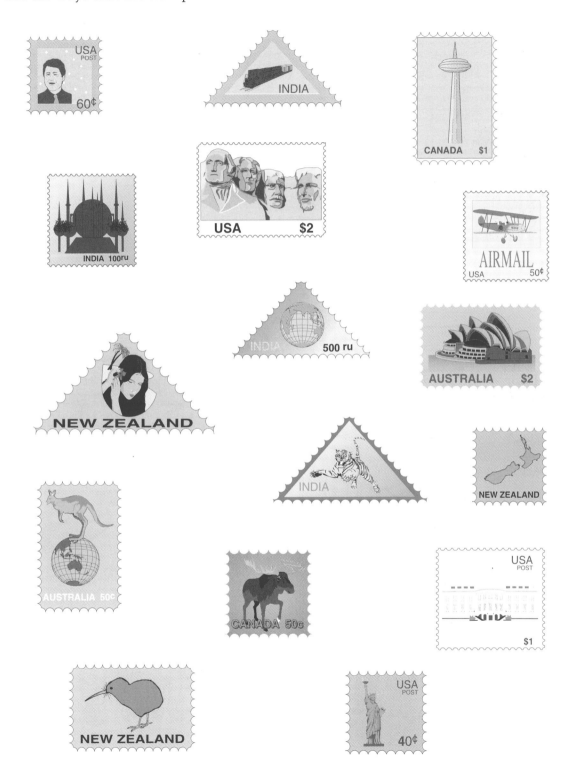

MORE THAN ONE CRITERIA

Exercise 7

Use the head sorter to match these dummies' heads to their correct bodies.

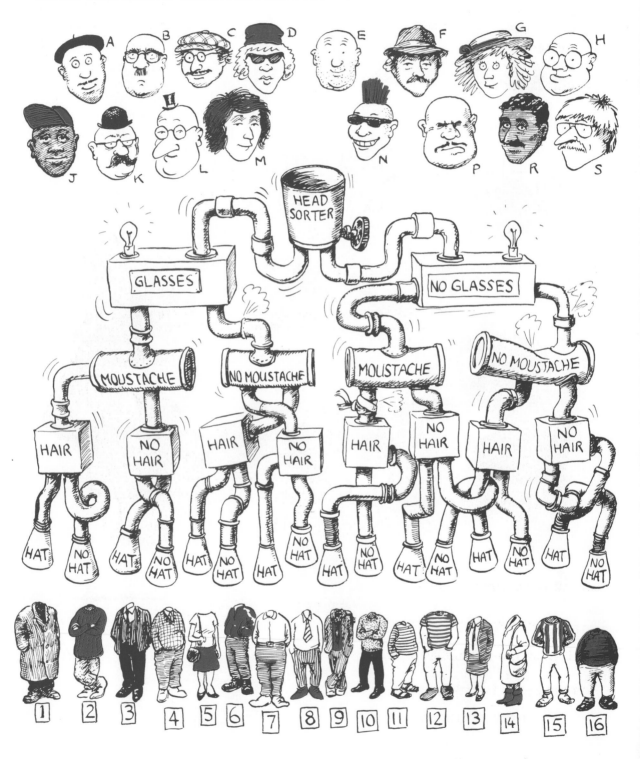

6 INTRODUCING DECIMALS

This unit will help you to:
→ **use a decimal point**
→ **understand decimal numbers**
→ **add and subtract decimal numbers**
→ **count on in tenths.**

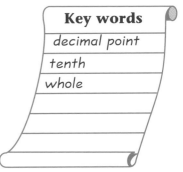

Key words

| decimal point |
| tenth |
| whole |

WHAT'S THE POINT?

The average number of children in a family is now officially 2.4.

NEWS

$2·4$ is a decimal number.

this is the decimal point.

2·4 is more than 2 and less than 3

You say **2·4** as **two** point **four**.

Exercise 1

1. Write these numbers in words:

    a 8·7   **b** 6·3   **c** 1·4   **d** 3·5   **e** 9·2

2. Write these numbers in digits:

    a two point six   **b** three point nine   **c** seven point eight

    d one point five   **e** nought point three

3. Copy and complete these sentences:

    a 12·6 is more than _____ and less than _13_ .

    b 6·6 is more than _6_ and less than _____ .

    c 1·7 is more than _____ and less than _____ .

    d 92·3 is more than _____ and less than _____ .

PARTS OF A WHOLE

The Declan Boys share one whole bar of chocolate.

They break the bar into **ten equal pieces**.

They get one piece each.

You use decimals to show parts of 1.

Each 1 is divided into 10 equal parts called **tenths**.

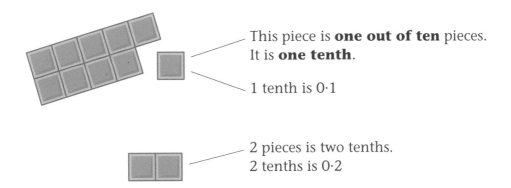

This piece is **one out of ten** pieces.
It is **one tenth**.

1 tenth is 0·1

2 pieces is two tenths.
2 tenths is 0·2

Exercise 2

1. How many tenths are there in each picture?

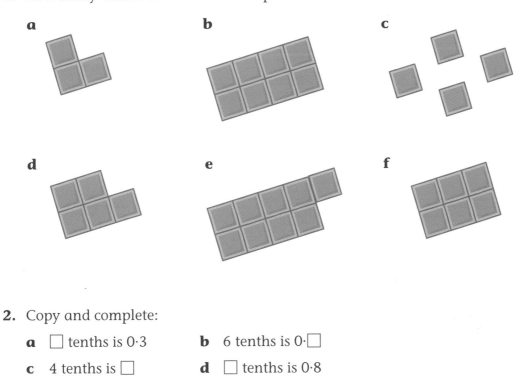

a **b** **c**

d **e** **f**

2. Copy and complete:

   a ☐ tenths is 0·3 **b** 6 tenths is 0·☐

   c 4 tenths is ☐ **d** ☐ tenths is 0·8

3. Are these shapes divided into tenths?
Answer Yes or No.

a 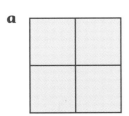 **b** 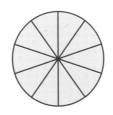 **c**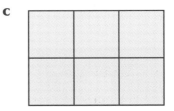

Exercise 3

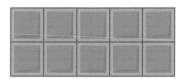

This is 1 whole or 1·0
It is split into tenths.
Each piece is 0·1.

In the drawing below what decimal part has been:

    a eaten   **b** left

Copy and complete the table.

The first one has been done for you:

1.    **2.**

3. 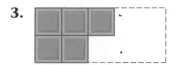   **4.**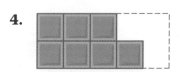

5.    **6.**

7.    **8.**

9. 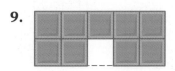   **10.**

	Eaten	Left
1.	0.1	0.9
2.		
3.		
4.		
5.		
6.		
7.		
8.		
9.		
10.		

Exercise 4

These rods are split into tenths.

a What decimal part of the rod is shaded?

b What decimal part of the rod is unshaded?

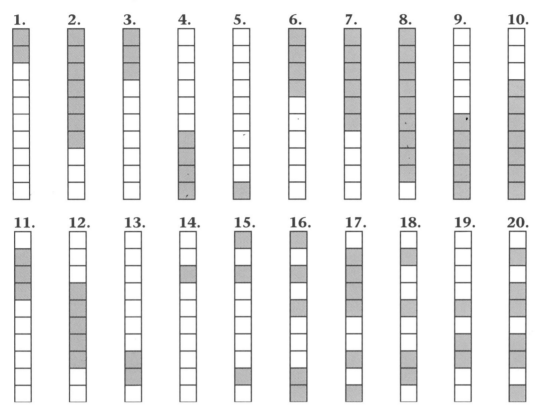

Exercise 5

These circles are split into ten equal parts.
What decimal part of each circle is

a shaded   **b** unshaded

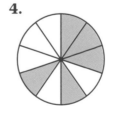
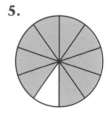
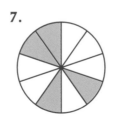
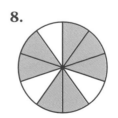
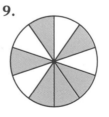
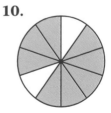

MORE THAN 1

Remember The decimal point separates the whole ones from the part less than one (tenths).

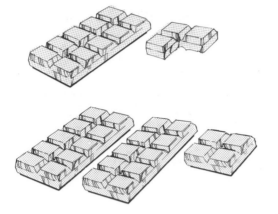

Here is 1 whole bar of chocolate and 3 tenths.

This is written 1·3.

Here are 2 whole bars and 4 tenths.

Exercise 6

Write down the number of bars of chocolate shown in each picture.
Remember to make the decimal point clear.

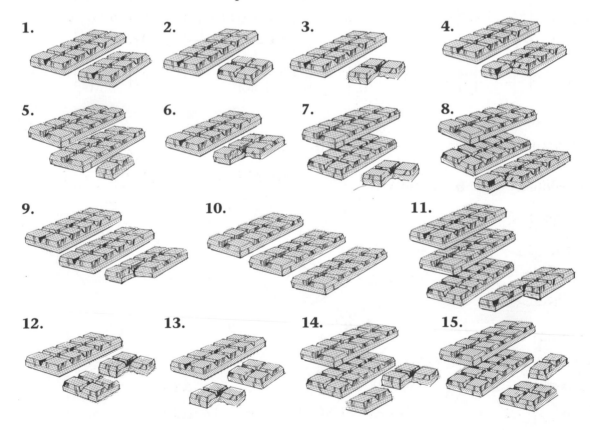

1.

2.

3.

4.

5.

6.

7.

8.

9.

10.

11.

12.

13.

14.

15.

ADDING AND SUBTRACTING DECIMALS

You can use simple drawings to show whole ones and tenths:

Use this rectangle to
represent a whole one

Use the small square to
represent a tenth

This drawing shows
2.3

You can use drawings to help you add decimal numbers like this:

0.3 + 0.4 = 0.7

1.2 + 0.4 = 1.6

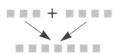

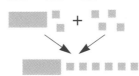

You can also subtract decimal numbers:

2.7 − 1.1 = 1.6

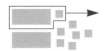

Exercise 7

Copy and complete these decimal calculations. You don't need to copy the pictures.

1. 0.4 + 0.4 =

2. 1.1 + 1.3 =

3. 2.2 + 0.7 =

4. 3.0 + 1.0 =

5. 1.6 + 1.3 =

6. 1.5 − 0.3 =

7. 2.7 − 1.6 =

8. 1.5 + 1.0 =

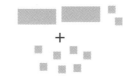

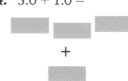

9. 0.6 + 0.4 =

10. 1.2 + 1.4 − 0.6 =

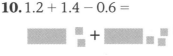

Exercise 8

Do these as quickly as you can.

1. a 3.1 + 2.6 =   **b** 4.0 + 3.7 =   **c** 5.1 + 0.8 =

2. a 3.9 − 2.6 =   **b** 4.8 − 3.6 =   **c** 6.7 − 2.5 =

MAKING A WHOLE

You can make a rectangle from 10 small squares: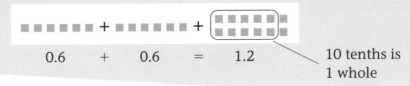

10 tenths make 1 whole one

Example 1

Work out 0.6 + 0.6

0.6   +   0.6   =   1.2   10 tenths is
                                   1 whole

Exercise 9

Add these amounts together. The pictures will help you.

1. 0.4 + 0.6 =

2.

3.

4.

5.

6.

LARGER NUMBERS

Example 2

Work out 2.3 + 1.8

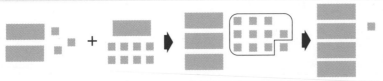

2.3   +   1.8   = 3 units + 11 tenths (1 whole and 1 tenth)
                        = 4 units + 1 tenth

2.3 + 1.8 = 4.1

Exercise 10

Add these amounts together. The pictures will help you.

1. 1.5 + 1.7 =

2. 2.5 + 3.7 =

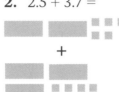

3. 1.8 + 0.9 =

4. 0.7 + 1.8 =

5. 2.1 + 1.6 =

6. 3.2 + 0.8 =

7. 0.4 + 3.7 =

8. 1.7 + 1.6 =

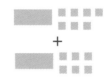

Exercise 11

The boxes below contain different decimal amounts of chocolate.
By adding or subtracting find ways of making up whole bars.

Like this: Box A + Box D: 1.6 + 0.4 = 2.0
You can use more than 2 boxes.

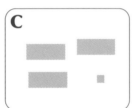

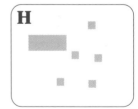

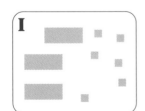

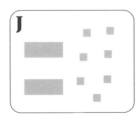

USING AN ABACUS

You can show decimal numbers on an abacus.

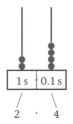

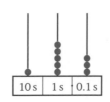

This abacus shows 2.4.   This abacus shows 15.3.

Exercise 12

Write down what decimal number each abacus shows:

1.   **2.**   **3.**   **4.**

            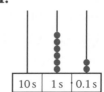

5.   **6.**   **7.**   **8.**

            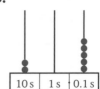

9. Show these numbers on an abacus.

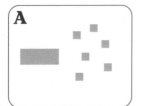         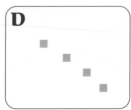

COUNTING IN TENTHS

You can use an abacus to count in tenths:

Example 3

Count on in tenths from 1.6:

1.6, 1.7, 1.8, ——, ——, ——,

Picture the abacus

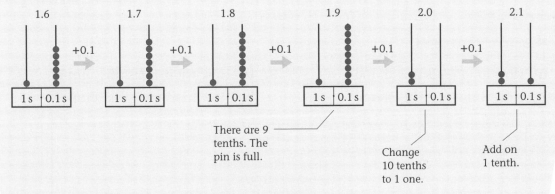

There are 9
tenths. The
pin is full.

Change
10 tenths
to 1 one.

Add on
1 tenth.

So the sequence goes 1.6, 1.7, 1.8, 1.9, 2.0, 2.1

Exercise 13

1. Use the picture of an abacus to count on:
   a   6.8, 6.9, 7.0 ——, ——, ——
   b   4.6, 4.7, 4.8, ——, ——, ——
   c   0.8, 0.9, ——, ——, ——
   d   2.6, 2.7, ——, ——, ——

2. Fill in the missing decimal numbers on these number lines:

   a   0.3   ?   ?   0.6   0.7   0.8   ?   ?   ?   1.2   ?

   b   ?   ?   0.9   ?   ?   1.2   1.3   1.4   ?   ?   ?

   c   4.6   4.7   4.8   ?   ?   ?   5.2   5.3   5.4   ?   ?

   d   ?   0.1   0.2   ?   0.4   ?   0.6   0.7   0.8   ?   ?

REVIEW 1

A. MEASUREMENT

1. Measure these lines.

a ├──────────────────────────────────────┤

b ├─────────────────────┤

c ├──────────────────────────────┤

d ├──────────┤

2. a How long (*e*) is this shape?

b How wide (*s*) is this shape?

3. a How wide (*m*) is this shape?

b How high (*r*) is this shape?

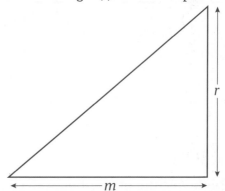

4. Which man is the tallest?
Use a ruler to check your answer.

5. Are these boxes all the same length?
If not which is different?

a 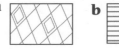   b   c

6. Which line is the longer, **a** or **b**?
Use your ruler to check your answer?

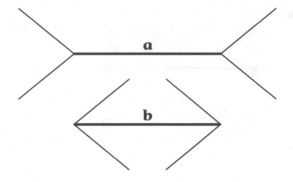

7. Are these two lines straight or crooked?
Check by measuring the distance between them at the top, the bottom and the middle.

8. Which circle is the bigger, **a** or **b**? Check your answer with a ruler.

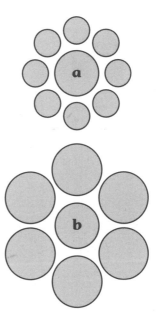

B. SHAPE

1. This shape is _____ .

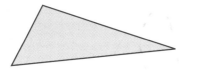

2. This shape is _____ .

3. This shape is _____ .

4. This shape is _____ .

5. What is this shape called?

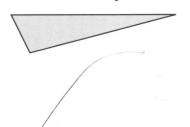

6. What is this shape called?

C. CIRCLES

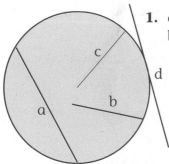

1. **a** Which line is a radius, **a**, **b**, **c** or **d**?
   b How long is the radius?

2. Using your compass, ruler and pencil draw a circle of radius 3 cm.

3. Now draw a circle of radius $4\frac{1}{2}$ cm.

4. Which line is a diameter, *r*, *s*, *t* or *u*?

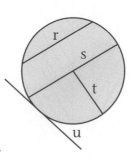

5. Draw a circle with a diameter of 8 cm.

D. SYMMETRY

1. Which lines of symmetry are correctly drawn?

a 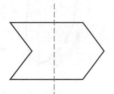   **b**   **c**

d 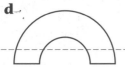   **e** 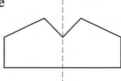   **f**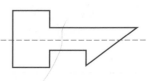

2. Copy these shapes. Draw lines of symmetry on them.

a    **b**   **c**   **d**

E. NUMBER

1.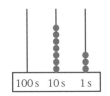

    a What number is shown on this abacus?

    b If you **add** 10 to this number, what will the total be?

    c If you **take away** 10 from this number, what will the total be?

2.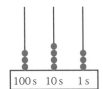

    a What number is shown on this abacus?

    b If you **add** 20 to this number, what will the total be?

    c If you **take away** 20 from this number, what will the total be?

Work these out in your head.

3. a 14 + 31   **b** 12 + 9   **c** 27 + 15   **d** 108 + 55

4. a 28 − 13   **b** 17 − 9   **c** 37 − 18   **d** 380 − 35

5. Match each decimal number with its drawing.

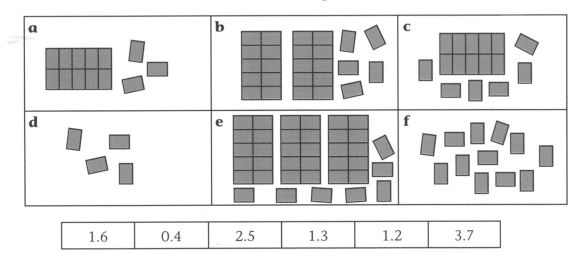

| 1.6 | 0.4 | 2.5 | 1.3 | 1.2 | 3.7 |

6. Write down the next three numbers in these sequences:

    a 1.6, 1.7, ——, ——, ——

    b 0.8, 0.9, ——, ——, ——

    c 9.7, 9.8, ——, ——, ——

7 NUMBER PATTERNS

This unit will help you to:
→ **find the next number in a number pattern**
→ **understand odd and even numbers.**

Key words

odd

even

pattern

JUMPS ON A NUMBER LINE

Jack is jumping along a number line on a pogo stick.

Exercise 1

Complete the drawings and the sentences.
The first one is done for you.

1.

The size of each jump is 1.
The next jump will land on 4.

2.

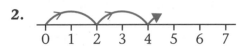

The size of each jump is ____
The next jump will land on ____

3.

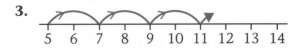

The size of each jump is ____
The next jump will land on ____

4.

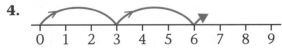

The size of each jump is ____
The next jump will land on ____

5.

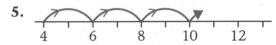

The size of each jump is ____
The next jump will land on ____

6.

The size of each jump is ____
The next jump will land on ____

7.

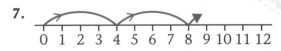

The size of each jump is ____
The next jump will land on ____

8.

The size of each jump is ____
The next jump will land on ____

Jack leaps from 2 on to 6 and then on to 10.

You can write his jumps like this:

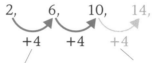

2,   6,   10,   14,

+4   +4   +4

He leaped 4 places each time.   He will land on 10 + 4 = 14 next.

Exercise 2

Here are Jack's jumps.
Write down **a** the size of each jump and **b** where he will land next.

1. 2, 4, 6, 8, ____   **2.** 3, 5, 7, 9, ____   **3.** 7, 9, 11, 13, ____

4. 11, 13, 15, 17, ____   **5.** 0, 3, 6, 9, ____   **6.** 1, 4, 7, 10, ____

7. 2, 5, 8, 11, ____   **8.** 4, 7, 10, 13, ____   **9.** 9, 12, 15, 18, ____

10. 6, 11, 16, 21, ____   **11.** 10, 16, 22, 28, ____   **12.** 4, 8, 12, 16 ____

Activity   DOUBLING PATTERNS

Each cockerel has two legs.

2 legs   4 legs   6 legs

1. If you know the number of cockerels, how do you find the number of legs?

2. Work out how many legs there will be when there are:
    a 5 cockerels   **b** 10 cockerels
    c 15 cockerels   **d** 25 cockerels

3. How many cockerels would there be if you could count 40 legs?

GOING BACKWARDS

Here Jack is jumping back along the number line.

Exercise 3

Complete the drawings and the sentences.
The first one is done for you.

1.

The size of each jump is 1.
The next jump will land on 2.

2.
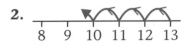

The size of each jump is ____
The next jump will land on ____

3.

The size of each jump is ____
The next jump will land on ____

4.

The size of each jump is ____
The next jump will land on ____

5.
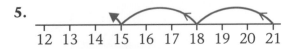

The size of each jump is ____
The next jump will land on ____

6.
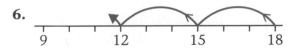

The size of each jump is ____
The next jump will land on ____

7.
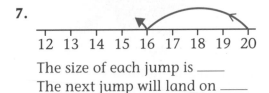

The size of each jump is ____
The next jump will land on ____

8.

The size of each jump is ____
The next jump will land on ____

9.
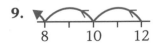

The size of each jump is ____
The next jump will land on ____

10.
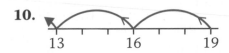

The size of each jump is ____
The next jump will land on ____

Jack is going back again. He starts at 22 and leaps back to 17 and then back to 12.

You can write his jump pattern like this:

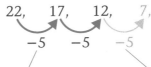

22,   17,   12,   7,

        −5   −5   −5

He moves 5 spaces   Next he will land on
backwards each time.   12 − 5 = 7.

Exercise 4

Here are Jack's jumps.
Write down **a** the size of each jump and **b** where he will land next.

1. 10, 8, 6, 4, ____   **2.** 15, 12, 9, 6, ____   **3.** 22, 20, 18, 16, ____

4. 9, 7, 5, 3, ____   **5.** 27, 25, 23, 21, ____   **6.** 13, 11, 9, 7, ____

7. 21, 18, 15, 12, ____   **8.** 17, 15, 13, 11, ____   **9.** 24, 20, 16, 12, ____

10. 40, 30, 20, 10, ____   **11.** 25, 20, 15, 10, ____   **12.** 17, 14, 11, 8, ____

ACTIVITY   DOUBLING, DOUBLING PATTERNS

Each deer has four legs.

4 legs   8 legs   12 legs

1. How do you calculate the number of legs if you know the number of deer?

2. Work out how many legs there will be when there are:

   a 5 deer   **b** 10 deer

   c 15 deer   **d** 25 deer

3. How many deer would there be if you could count 40 legs?

ODD AND EVEN NUMBERS

Clare and Shopna are building a simple
bench using a plank of wood and blocks.

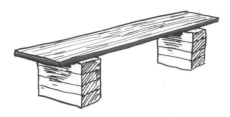

As they build the bench they notice something.

When they use 1 block, 3 blocks or 5 blocks the bench looks 'odd'.
1, 3 and 5 are ODD numbers.
2, 4 and 6 are EVEN numbers.

Exercise 5

1. Copy and continue the pattern of odd numbers up to 15.

1, 3, 5, ——, ——, ——, ——, 15.

2. Copy and continue the pattern of even numbers up to 20.

2, 4, 6, ——, ——, ——, ——, ——, ——, 20

3. Sort these numbers into two groups: ODD and EVEN.

7	10	13	5	20	
11			14		22
	9		1	16	
8	6	3	15	19	

EVEN numbers can be split into 2 equal piles
　　2, 4, 6, 8, 10, 12, ... are all EVEN numbers

ODD numbers cannot be split into 2 equal piles
　　1, 3, 5, 7, 9, 11, ... are all ODD numbers

Activity

1. Choose two **even** numbers. Add them together.
    Is the total odd or even?
    Choose more pairs of even numbers and add them.

    Which sentence is true? Choose **a**, **b** or **c**.
    a　The answer is always an odd number.
    b　The answer is always an even number.
    c　The answer is sometimes odd and sometimes even.

2. Choose two **odd** numbers. Add them together.
    Is the total odd or even?
    Choose more pairs of odd numbers and add them.

    Which sentence is true? Choose **a**, **b** or **c**.
    a　The answer is always an odd number.
    b　The answer is always an even number.
    c　The answer is sometimes odd and sometimes even.

3. Choose one **odd** number and one **even** number. Add them together.
    Is the total odd or even?
    Choose more pairs of odd and even numbers and add them.

    Which sentence is true? Choose **a**, **b** or **c**.
    a　The answer is always an odd number.
    b　The answer is always an even number.
    c　The answer is sometimes odd and sometimes even.

In the pattern of even numbers up to 30:

　　2, 4, 6, 8, 10, 12, 14, 16, 18, 20, 22, 24, 26, 28, 30

the units digit is either 2, 4, 6, 8 or 0.

Remember　Even numbers have a units digit of 2, 4, 6, 8 or 0.
　　　　　　　Odd numbers have a units digit of 1, 3, 5, 7 or 9.

Exercise 6

Which of these number are odd and which are even?

1. 81	**2.** 64	**3.** 143	**4.** 479	**5.** 862
6. 100	**7.** 227	**8.** 392	**9.** 527	**10.** 9152

8 THE FOUR RULES OF NUMBER

This unit will help you to:
→ **revise addition and subtraction techniques**
→ **multiply small numbers**
→ **divide by sharing**
→ **understand the symbols ×, ÷.**

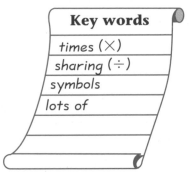

Key words

times (×)
sharing (÷)
symbols
lots of

REVISING ADDITION

Remember: thinking of a number line can help you add in your head.

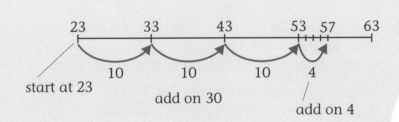

Example 1
Work out 23 + 34.

start at 23

23 + 34 = 57   add on 30

add on 4

Do the following questions in your head as quickly as you can.
Use a number line if you need help.

Addition workcard 1

1. 26 + 40 =	**2.** 30 + 50 =	**3.** 40 + 30 =	**4.** 35 + 15 =
5. 17 + 23 =	**6.** 30 + 60 =	**7.** 21 + 39 =	**8.** 10 + 50 =
9. 62 + 28 =	**10.** 14 + 26 =	**11.** 33 + 27 =	**12.** 19 + 51 =

Addition workcard 2

1. 5 + 27 =	**2.** 72 + 90 =	**3.** 65 + 19 =	**4.** 37 + 36 =
5. 38 + 4 =	**6.** 18 + 43 =	**7.** 49 + 6 =	**8.** 7 + 25 =
9. 55 + 8 =	**10.** 8 + 54 =	**11.** 39 + 41 =	**12.** 74 + 6 =

Addition workcard 3

1. 122 + 1 + 14 =	**2.** 23 + 10 + 6 =	**3.** 34 + 14 + 21 =	**4.** 26 + 2 + 11
5. 14 + 20 + 15 =	**6.** 30 + 11 + 27 =	**7.** 25 + 5 + 20 =	**8.** 16 + 12 + 8 =
9. 24 + 16 + 7 =	**10.** 8 + 12 + 25 =	**11.** 26 + 16 + 25 =	**12.** 13 + 18 + 36 =

SUBTRACTION

These words normally mean subtract:

how many left?   take away   minus

Exercise 1

See how many questions you can do in 30 minutes.

1. If you took 2 apples from this tray, how many would be left?

2. If you took 5 sweets from this tray, how many would be left?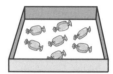

3. If you took 4 mushrooms from this tray, how many would be left?

4. If you took 3 boxes from this tray, how many would be left?

5. If you took 7 stamps from this sheet of, stamps, how many would be left?

6. If you took 5 stamps from this sheet of, stamps, how many would be left?

7. If you took 4 stamps from this sheet of, stamps, how many would be left?

8. If you took 8 stamps from this sheet of, stamps, how many would be left?

Copy and complete these.

9. 6 take away 2 is ____

10. 8 minus 5 is ____

11. 9 take away 1 equals ____

12. 7 minus 6 equals ____

13. 5 take away 5 is ____

14. 10 minus 5 is ____

15. 10 minus 1 equals ____

16. 12 take away 6 equals ____

17. 13 take away 3 is ____

18. 11 take away 5 makes ____

19. 9 take away 7 is ____

20. 12 subtract 10 equals ____

21. There are 15 toffees in this bag.

Ben eats 3 and Judy eats 4; how many are left?

There are ____ toffees left.

22. Steven has 17 comics. He gives 5 of them to Lenny and 2 to Bob. How many comics has he got left?

Steven has ____ comics left.

SUBTRACTING IN YOUR HEAD

Here are two methods for subtracting in your head:

Method 1
Counting on.

Method 2
Counting back.

Choose the method you prefer and use it to work out these subtraction sums:

Subtraction workcard 1

1. 30 − 17 =   **2.** 40 − 18 =   **3.** 50 − 16 =   **4.** 60 − 15 =

5. 80 − 19 =   **6.** 40 − 14 =   **7.** 30 − 13 =   **8.** 50 − 12 =

Subtraction workcard 2

1. 60 − 37 =   **2.** 50 − 24 =   **3.** 70 − 23 =   **4.** 60 − 45 =

5. 90 − 27 =   **6.** 40 − 26 =   **7.** 40 − 13 =   **8.** 100 − 42 =

Subtraction workcard 3

1. 32 − 17 =   **2.** 51 − 18 =   **3.** 44 − 16 =   **4.** 73 − 15 =

5. 48 − 19 =   **6.** 51 − 14 =   **7.** 61 − 13 =   **8.** 71 − 12 =

Subtraction workcard 4

1. 63 − 37 =   **2.** 47 − 24 =   **3.** 51 − 23 =   **4.** 82 − 45 =

5. 45 − 27 =   **6.** 74 − 26 =   **7.** 41 − 13 =   **8.** 98 − 49 =

Exercise 2

Do these in your head as quickly as you can. Give yourself 15 minutes!
The first one is done for you.

1.

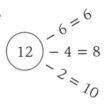

12
− 6 = 6
− 4 = 8
− 2 = 10

2.

15
− 5 = □
− 12 = □
− 4 = □

3.

10
− 9 = □
− 4 = □
− 1 = □

4.

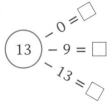

13
− 0 = □
− 9 = □
− 13 = □

5.

11
− 2 = □
− 7 = □
− 9 = □

6.

27
− 11 = □
− 24 = □
− 20 = □

7.

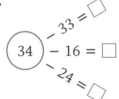

34
− 33 = □
− 16 = □
− 24 = □

8.

30
− 17 = □
− 30 = □
− 21 = □

9.

43
− 16 = □
− 24 = □
− 26 = □

Exercise 3

The scales in each picture will not balance because there is a weight missing from one side. Work out how much you need to add to make the scales balance.

1.

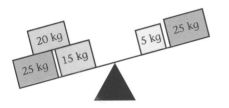

2.

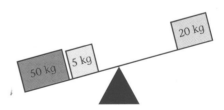

3.

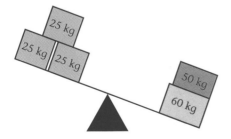

4.

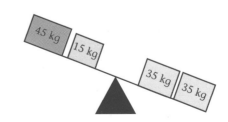

LOTS OF PIGS

Farmer Jones has 4 stalls. In each stall there are 3 pigs.
To find out how many pigs he has, Farmer Jones adds 4 lots of pigs:

$$3 + 3 + 3 + 3 = 12$$

Exercise 4

Write out these problems in the same way as Farmer Jones.
The first one is done for you.

1. 3 lots of 5 = 5 + 5 + 5 = 15   **2.** 2 lots of 5   **3.** 5 lots of 2

4. 3 lots of 2   **5.** 4 lots of 3   **6.** 2 lots of 6

7. 5 lots of 3   **8.** 2 lots of 7   **9.** 4 lots of 4

10. 6 lots of 3   **11.** 4 lots of 2   **12.** 6 lots of 2

Use a short cut to find an answer to these

13. 10 lots of 4   **14.** 10 lots of 7   **15.** 10 lots of 9

16. 20 lots of 3   **17.** 20 lots of 5   **18.** 20 lots of 4

19. 30 lots of 2   **20.** 30 lots of 6   **21.** 30 lots of 8

TIMES

Farmer Jones has 4 lots of 3 pigs.

You can write $3 + 3 + 3 + 3$

          as 4×3 ——————— You say 'four times three'.

4×3 means 4 times 3   or   4 lots of 3.

Exercise 5

Write these sums using $\times$.
The first one is done for you.

1. $6 + 6 + 6 = 3 \times 6$

2. $5 + 5 + 5 + 5$

3. $3 + 3$

4. $4 + 4 + 4 + 4 + 4$

5. $7 + 7 + 7 + 7$

6. $8 + 8 + 8$

7. $2 + 2 + 2 + 2 + 2 + 2$

8. $3 + 3 + 3 + 3 + 3$

9. $7 + 7 + 7 + 7 + 7 + 7$

Exercise 6

Write these sums out in full.
The first one is done for you.

1. $6 \times 7 = 7 + 7 + 7 + 7 + 7 + 7$

2. 5×3

3. 4×8

4. 3×8

5. 6×2

6. 8×3

7. 10×4

8. 7×5

9. 1×7

Exercise 7

Each pen holds the same number of pigs,
but how many pigs are there in each pen?

1.  = 16

2.  = 21

3.  = 24

4.  = 40

5.  = 30

6. 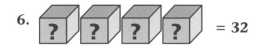 = 32

TWO TIMES

You can use a number line to work out answers:

Example 2
Work out 5×2

5×2 is 5 lots of 2   or   5 jumps of 2:

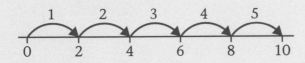

5 jumps of 2 makes 10.

So $5 \times 2 = 10$.

Exercise 8

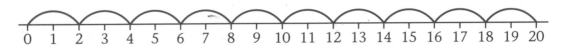

1. What do 3 jumps of 2 make?   2. What do 2 jumps of 2 make?

3. What do 5 jumps of 2 make?   4. What do 6 jumps of 2 make?

5. What do 9 jumps of 2 make?   6. What do 8 jumps of 2 make?

7. There are 2 beads in each tin.
   How many beads are there in 7 tins?

8. There are 2 people in each car.
   How many people are there in 5 cars?

Use the number line to solve these problems.

9. **a** $1 \times 2 = \square$ **b** $3 \times 2 = \square$ **c** $5 \times 2 = \square$ **d** $4 \times 2 = \square$

   e $6 \times 2 = \square$ **f** $8 \times 2 = \square$ **g** $7 \times 2 = \square$ **h** $10 \times 2 = \square$

10. Copy and complete the **2 times table**:

    2, 4, 6, 8, ____ , ____ , ____ , ____ , ____ , ____

THREE TIMES

This number line shows jumps of 3.

Exercise 9

1. What do 3 jumps of 3 make?   **2.** What do 2 jumps of 3 make?

3. What do 6 jumps of 3 make?   **4.** What do 8 jumps of 3 make?

5. Here are 4 plates. On each plate there are 3 eggs. How many eggs are there in total?

6. Here are 5 pods. There are 3 peas in each pod. How many peas are there in all?

7. There are 3 holes in each button. There are 8 buttons. How many holes are there?

8. There are 3 sweets in each box. How many sweets in 4 boxes?

9. There are 3 apples in each tin. How many apples in 7 tins?

10. Use the number line to copy and complete:

   a $1 \times 3 = \square$ **b** $3 \times 3 = \square$ **c** $\square \times 3 = 12$ **d** $\square \times 3 = 27$ **e** $6 \times 3 = \square$

11. Copy and complete the **3 times table**:

   3, 6, 9, 12, ____, ____, ____, ____, ____, ____

FOUR TIMES

This number line shows jumps of 4.

Exercise 10

1. What do 1 jumps of 4 make?   **2.** What do 3 jumps of 4 make?

3. What do 4 jumps of 4 make?   **4.** What do 8 jumps of 4 make?

5. Here are 5 plates. On each plate there are 4 eggs. How many eggs are there in total?

6. Here are 4 candles on each cake. There are 7 cakes. How many candles are there in total?

7. There are 4 cakes in each pack. How many cakes in 3 packs?

8. There are 4 biscuits in each box. How many are there in 6 boxes?

9. Use the number line to copy and complete:

   a $2 \times 4 = \square$ **b** $8 \times 4 = \square$ **c** $\square \times 4 = 12$ **d** $\square \times 4 = 24$ **e** $10 \times 4 = \square$

10. Copy and complete the **4 times table**:

   4, 8, 12, ____, ____, ____, ____, ____, ____, ____

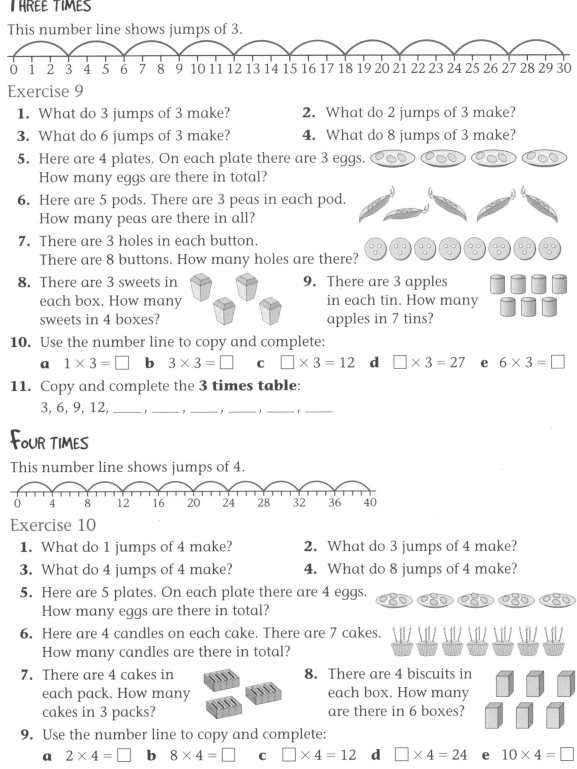

FIVE TIMES

This number line shows jumps of 5.

Exercise 11

1. What do 3 jumps of 5 make?   2. What do 5 jumps of 5 make?

3. What do 7 jumps of 5 make?   4. What do 10 jumps of 5 make?

5. Here are 5 necklaces. On each necklace there are 5 pearls.
   How many pearls are there in total?

6. Here are 5 cakes in each box. There are 6 boxes.
   How many cakes are there?

7. Here are 8 bags. There are 5 apples in each bag.
   How many apples are there in total?

8. There are 5 sweets in
   each pack. How many
   sweets in 2 packs?

9. There are 5 eggs in
   each box. How many
   eggs in 4 boxes?

10. Use the number line to copy and complete:
    a $3 \times 5 = \square$ **b** $8 \times 5 = \square$ **c** $\square \times 5 = 10$ **d** $\square \times 5 = 35$ **e** $5 \times 5 = \square$

11. Copy and complete the **5 times table**:
    5, 10, 15, ____, ____, ____, ____, ____, ____, ____

TEN TIMES

This number line shows jumps of 10.

Exercise 12

1. What do 3 jumps of 10 make?   2. What do 5 jumps of 10 make?

3. What do 6 jumps of 10 make?   4. What do 9 jumps of 10 make?

5. Here are 4 trays. There are 10 biscuits on each tray.
   How many biscuits are there in all?

6. Here are 8 cards. There are 10 buttons on each card.
   How many buttons are there in total?

7. There are 10 plums in
   each tin. How many
   plums in 3 tins?

8. There are 10 stones in
   each pot. How many
   stones in 7 pots?

9. Use the number line to copy and complete:
   a $4 \times 10 = \square$ **b** $8 \times 10 = \square$ **c** $\square \times 10 = 60$ **d** $\square \times 10 = 50$ **e** $10 \times 10 = \square$

10. Copy and complete the **10 times table**:
    10, 20, ____, ____, ____, ____, ____, ____, ____, ____

SHARING IT OUT

Farmer Jones has 15 hens. He wants to share the hens equally between 3 hen houses.
15 shared between 3 = 5.
So there will be 5 hens in each hen house.

Exercise 13

Copy and complete these sentences. The first one is done for you.

1. 6 shared between 2 is 3

2. 8 shared between 4 is ____

3. 8 shared between 2 is ____

4. 12 shared between 3 is ____

5. 10 shared between 2 is ____

6. 6 shared between 3 is ____

7. 10 shared between 5 is ____

8. 14 shared between 7 is ____

9. 9 shared between 9 is ____

Exercise 14

Sharing in 3s

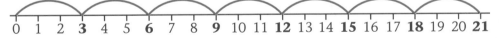

1. How many groups of 3 will you have in 9?

2. How many groups of 3 will you have in 15?

3. How many groups of 3 will you have in 6?

4. How many groups of 3 will you have in 21?

5. How many groups of 3 will you have in 18?

6. Share 12 dots into 4 groups.
How many dots are there
in each group?

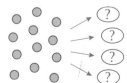

Exercise 15
Sharing in 4s

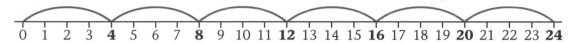

1. How many groups of 4 will you have in 8?

2. How many groups of 4 will you have in 16?

3. How many groups of 4 will you have in 12?

4. How many groups of 4 will you have in 24?

5. How many groups of 4 will you have in 20?

6. Share 20 squares into 5 groups. How many squares are there in each group?

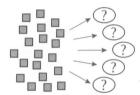

Exercise 16
Sharing in 5s

1. How many groups of 5 will you have in 15?

2. How many groups of 5 will you have in 20?

3. How many groups of 5 will you have in 10?

4. How many groups of 5 will you have in 30?

5. How many groups of 5 will you have in 25?

6. Share the 15 crosses into 3 groups. How many crosses are there in each group?

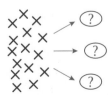

Exercise 17

1. Share these 6 apples between 2 baskets.

How many apples in each basket?

2. Share these 9 sweets  between 3 children.

How many sweets each?

3. Share these 12 beads  between 4 tins.

How many beads in each tin?

4. Share these 10 buns between 2 boxes.

How many buns in each box?

5. Share these 16 coins between 4 children.

How many coins each?

DIVIDING

You can write 15 shared between 3 = 5

as 15   ÷   3 = 5

÷ symbol means 'shared between'   or   'divided by'

Exercise 18
Copy and complete:

1. 9 ÷ 3 =   **2.** 8 ÷ 4 =   **3.** 6 ÷ 2 =

4. 10 ÷ 2 =   **5.** 12 ÷ 4 =   **6.** 15 ÷ 5 =

7. 14 ÷ 2 =   **8.** 18 ÷ 2 =   **9.** 16 ÷ 4 =

10. 20 ÷ 5 =   **11.** 18 ÷ 6 =   **12.** 20 ÷ 10 =

Exercise 19

Here is a code table. Each letter has a number code.

A	B	C	D	E	F	G	H	I	J	K	L	M
24	39	21	8	**13**	14	1	**18**	16	23	4	11	20

N	O	P	Q	R	S	T	U	V	W	X	Y	Z
30	2	6	5	25	9	**7**	15	19	3	12	17	28

Work out the answers. Then work out the message.
The first one is done for you.

$(4 + 3 = \textbf{7:T})$ $(6 \times 3 = \textbf{18:H})$ $(19 - 6 = \textbf{13:E}) = $ THE

$(10 \div 2 = \square)$ $(5 \times 3 = \square)$ $(27 - 11 = \square)$ $(12 + 9 = \square)$ $(12 \div 3 = \square) = $ ____

$(8 + 31 = \square)$ $(5 \times 5 = \square)$ $(17 - 15 = \square)$ $(6 \div 2 = \square)$ $(10 \times 3 = \square) = $ ____

$(21 - 7 = \square)$ $(20 \div 10 = \square)$ $(6 + 6 = \square) = $ ____

$(12 + 11 = \square)$ $(20 - 5 = \square)$ $(4 \times 5 = \square)$ $(12 \div 2 = \square)$ $(3 \times 3 = \square) = $ ____

$(2 \times 1 = \square)$ $(9 + 10 = \square)$ $(26 \div 2 = \square)$ $(9 + 16 = \square) = $ ____

$(14 \div 2 = \square)$ $(9 + 9 = \square)$ $(13 + 0 = \square) = $ ____

$(17 - 6 = \square)$ $(8 \times 3 = \square)$ $(4 \times 7 = \square)$ $(4 + 13 = \square) = $ ____

$(16 \div 2 = \square)$ $(31 - 29 = \square)$ $(17 - 16 = \square) = $ ____

Exercise 20

Put this sentence into code using the code table from Exercise 18.

The noisy noise annoys an oyster.

MIXED PROBLEMS

Remember: + means add   − means take away   × means times   ÷ means divide

Exercise 21

Copy out these problems and put the right sign in place of $\square$.

1. $3 \square 2 = 5$ **2.** $6 \square 2 = 4$ **3.** $3 \square 2 = 6$ **4.** $8 \square 3 = 5$

5. $8 \square 2 = 4$ **6.** $3 \square 3 = 9$ **7.** $8 \square 4 = 12$ **8.** $6 \square 2 = 3$

9. $9 \square 1 = 8$ **10.** $5 \square 2 = 10$ **11.** $10 \square 2 = 5$ **12.** $6 \square 5 = 11$

13. $8 \square 2 = 6$ **14.** $3 \square 4 = 12$ **15.** $8 \square 9 = 17$ **16.** $8 \square 2 = 16$

17. $8 \square 4 = 2$ **18.** $4 \square 4 = 16$ **19.** $9 \square 3 = 6$ **20.** $4 \square 16 = 20$

21. $6 \square 8 = 14$ **22.** $5 \square 3 = 15$ **23.** $9 \square 3 = 3$ **24.** $9 \square 9 = 0$

Exercise 22

Which door does each route bring you to?

9 MONEY

This unit will help you to:
- → **recognise coins and notes**
- → **write money amounts**
- → **add money amounts**
- → **work out how much change you should get.**

Key words

coins/notes
expensive
cheapest

MONEY, MONEY, MONEY

These are all the different coins and notes used in the UK.

Coins	**Notes**

1p
penny

2p
Two pence

5p
Five pence

10p
Ten pence

20p
Twenty pence

50p
Fifty pence

£1
One pound coin

£2
Two pound coin

£5
Five pound note

£10
Ten
pound note

£20
Twenty
pound note

£50
Fifty
pound note

You write small amounts of money in pence.

Example 1
Here is 17p

Exercise 1
How much money is there in each box?

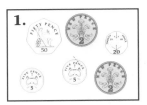   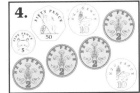

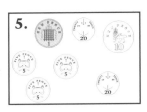   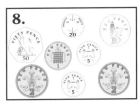

Exercise 2

1. If you had 4 , how much would you have?

2. If you had 5 , how much would you have?

3. If you had 3 , how much would you have?

4. If you had 7 , how much would you have?

5. If you had 4 , how much would you have?

6. If you had 12 , how much would you have?

7. If you had 8 , how much would you have?

8. If you had 4 , how much would you have?

9. If you had 25 , how much would you have?

10. If you had 3 and 3 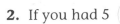 , how much would you have?

You write whole pounds using the symbol £.

Example 2

This is £3 altogether.

Exercise 3

How much money is in each box?

1.

2.

3.

4.

5.

6.

7.

8.

Exercise 4

Here are some items for sale in a shop:

What is the cost of:

1. Two packets of gum.

2. A bag of crisps and a pack of gum.

3. A pack of chews and a pack of gum.

4. A bag of crisps and a bar of chocolate.

5. A bar of chocolate and a pack of chews.

6. A can of lemonade and a bag of crisps.

7. A bar of chocolate and a can of lemonade.

8. A bar of toffee and a pack of gum.

9. Two bars of chocolate and a pack of crisps.

10. A bar of toffee and a can lemonade.

11. A pack of gum and two bags of crisps.

12. Two cans of lemonade.

13. Two packets of chews and a pack of gum.

14. Two bags of crisps and a bar of chocolate.

Exercise 5

Copy and complete these sentences.

1. There are ____ 10p pieces in £1.00.

2. There are ____ 2p pieces in 10p.

3. There are ____ 5p pieces in 20p.

4. There are ____ 5p pieces in 50p.

5. There are ____ 50p pieces in £2.00.

6. There are ____ 5p pieces in £1.00.

7. There are ____ 2p pieces in 20p.

8. There are ____ 20p pieces in £1.00.

9. There are ____ 20p pieces in £1.60.

10. There are ____ 10p pieces in £1.40.

11. There are ____ 5p pieces in 45p.

12. There are ____ 2p pieces in 34p.

HOW MUCH CHANGE?

This bubble bath costs £2.25.

£2.25 is £2 and 25 pence.

The point separates the pounds from the pence.

You need to be able to work out how much change you will get.

Example 3

If you paid for the bubble bath with a £5 note how much change would you get?

Add on from £2 and 25 pence

add on to make the next whole pound ▼ + 75 pence

£3

add on to make five pounds: ▼ + £2

£5

So you would get £2.75 change.

Exercise 6

How much change would you get if you paid these bills with a £5 note?

1.	£4.50	**2.**	£3.70	**3.**	£1.90	**4.**	£2.15
5.	£4.28	**6.**	£3.76	**7.**	£2.11	**8.**	£1.66

POUNDS OR PENCE?

You can write money amounts in pounds and pence.

Remember: there are 100p in £1.

Example 4

a Write £2.36 in pence.

a £2.36 is £2 and 36p

£2 is 200p

So £2.36 is 236p.

b Write 173p in pounds.

b 173p is 100p and 73p

100p is £1

So 173p is £1.73

Exercise 7

1. Write these amounts in pence.

a	£2.17	**b**	£1.92	**c**	£7.75	**d**	£8.99
e	£5.50	**f**	£6.05	**g**	£8.00	**h**	£11.22

2. Write these amounts in pounds.

a	186p	**b**	392p	**c**	617p	**d**	520p
e	1619p	**f**	805p	**g**	900p	**h**	67p

EARNING POCKET MONEY

To earn their pocket money Jenny and Mark have to help with the housework.
In the kitchen is a chart which says how much they can earn for each task

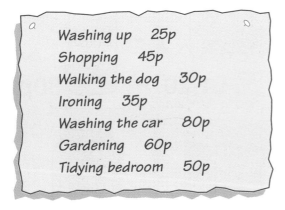

Washing up   25p
Shopping   45p
Walking the dog   30p
Ironing   35p
Washing the car   80p
Gardening   60p
Tidying bedroom   50p

Exercise 8

Their mother keeps a record of the tasks Jenny and Mark do during each week.
Each time a task is done she puts a tick on the chart. Here is the chart for one week.

Copy and complete these sentences.

1. Jenny earned ____ washing up.
2. Mark earned ____ shopping.
3. Jenny earned ____ walking the dog.
4. Jenny earned ____ tidying the bedroom.
5. Jenny earned 70p from ____ .
6. Mark earned £1.50 from ____ .
7. Jenny earned £ ____ in all.
8. Mark earned £ ____ in all.

Task	Jenny	Mark
Washing up	✓✓✓	✓✓
Shopping	✓✓✓	✓✓✓
Walking the dog	✓✓	✓✓✓
Ironing	✓✓	✓
Washing the car	✓	✓
Gardening	✓	✓
Tidying bedroom	✓✓	✓✓✓

Exercise 9

Each week Jenny and Mark save £1.40.
Copy and complete their savings record chart.
Jenny started with savings of £1.20 and Mark started with 90p.

	Week One	Week Two	Week Three	Week Four	Week Five	Week Six	Week Seven	Week Eight	Week Nine	Week Ten
Jenny	£1.20		£4.00				£9.60			£13.80
Mark	90p	£2.30			£6.50				£12.10	

MORE SHOPPING

Dennisons **Beans** — 21p

BOURBON BUSCUITS — 35p

CORN FLAKES — £1·20

Washing up LIQUID — 80p

TEA BAGS — £1·10

Orange juice — 72p

KITCHEN ROLL — 95p

INSTANT COFFEE — £2·30

SUGAR 1kg — 51p

Crisps — 25p

Peas — 15p

6 eggs — 60p

Fish fingers — 99p

WHITE Bread — 54p

SOFT BUTTER — 70p

RICE 25% extra free — 65p

SPIT MATCHES — 12p

COOL FRESH MILK — 30p

CHICKEN SOUP — 25p

BEEF BURGERS — £1·50

Exercise 10

1. Which item is the most expensive?

2. Which item is the cheapest?

3. Which item costs 80p?

4. If you bought a pack of eggs, how much change would you get from £1?

5. If you bought a pack of kitchen roll, how much change would you get from £1?

6. If you bought a jar of instant coffee, how much change would you get from £5?

7. **a** How much will a tin of beans and a tin of peas cost?
   b How much change from 50p would you expect if you bought them?

8. **a** How much will a tin of soup and a carton of milk cost?
   b How much change would you get from £1?

9. **a** How much will a pack of beefburgers and a pack of eggs cost?
   b How much change would you get from £5?

10. **a** How much will a bag of crisps, a bag of sugar and a loaf of bread cost?
    b How much change would you get from £2?

11. How many boxes of tea-bags can be bought with £5?

12. How many boxes of matches can be bought with 50p?

13. Buy the items you would need to make a cup of tea.
    How much do they cost in total?

14. You are going to make breakfast.
    a List the things you will buy.
    b How much do they cost in total?

15. How much will each of these shopping lists add up to?

a
Pack of tea
Pack of biscuits
Bag of rice
Carton of milk

b
3 bags of crisps
Pack of fish fingers
Tin of peas

c
Bottle of washing up liquid
Tin of beans
2 tins of soup

d If each bill is paid with a £10 note, what will be the change each time?

10 TIME

This unit will help you to:
→ **know the months of the year**
→ **use a calendar**
→ **read clocks**
→ **work with timetables**
→ **use a.m. and p.m.**

Key words

calendar
season
analogue
digital
fast/slow

THE FOUR SEASONS

The year is divided into four seasons: Spring, Summer, Autumn, Winter.
The seasons change in the middle of certain months.

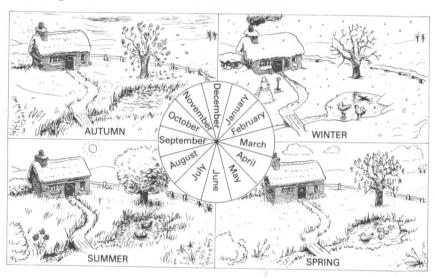

Exercise 1

Copy and complete this sentence for each of the season changes:

The season changes from _____ to _____ in the month of _____ .

Exercise 2

Which season is most appropriate for the following?

1. Very long nights and short days.
2. Sun tan oil.
3. The season after Summer.
4. Flowers and trees start growing again.
5. Ice and snow.
6. The season that follows Winter.
7. The hottest season.
8. The season in which Christmas falls.
9. Trees lose their leaves.
10. The season you were born in.

Using a calendar

Here is the calendar for 2001.

	January					February						March						April			
Sunday		7	14	21	28		4	11	18	25		4	11	18	25	1	8	15	22	29	
Monday	1	8	15	22	29		5	12	19	26		5	12	19	26	2	9	16	23	30	
Tuesday	2	9	16	23	30		6	13	20	27		6	13	20	27	3	10	17	24		
Wednesday	3	10	17	24	31		7	14	21	28		7	14	21	28	4	11	18	25		
Thursday	4	11	18	25		1	8	15	22		1	8	15	22	29	5	12	19	26		
Friday	5	12	19	26		2	9	16	23		2	9	16	23	30	6	13	20	27		
Saturday	6	13	20	27		3	10	17	24		3	10	17	24	31	7	14	21	28		

	May					June					July					August			
Sunday		6	13	20	27		3	10	17	24	1	8	15	22	29		5	12	19	26
Monday		7	14	21	28		4	11	18	25	2	9	16	23	30		6	13	20	27
Tuesday	1	8	15	22	29		5	12	19	26	3	10	17	24	31		7	14	21	28
Wednesday	2	9	16	23	30		6	13	20	27	4	11	18	25		1	8	15	22	29
Thursday	3	10	17	24	31		7	14	21	28	5	12	19	26		2	9	16	23	30
Friday	4	11	18	25		1	8	15	22	29	6	13	20	27		3	10	17	24	31
Saturday	5	12	19	26		2	9	16	23	30	7	14	21	28		4	11	18	25	

	September					October					November					December				
Sunday		2	9	16	23	30		7	14	21	28		4	11	18	25		2	9	16	23	30
Monday		3	10	17	24		1	8	15	22	29		5	12	19	26		3	10	17	24	31
Tuesday		4	11	18	25		2	9	16	23	30		6	13	20	27		4	11	18	25
Wednesday		5	12	19	26		3	10	17	24	31		7	14	21	28		5	12	19	26
Thursday		6	13	20	27		4	11	18	25		1	8	15	22	29		6	13	20	27
Friday		7	14	21	28		5	12	19	26		2	9	16	23	30		7	14	21	28
Saturday	1	8	15	22	29		6	13	20	27		3	10	17	24		1	8	15	22	29

Exercise 3

Use the calendar above to complete the sentences below.

1. The first month of the year is _____.
2. The sixth month of the year is _____.
3. The tenth month of the year is _____.
4. There are _____ months in a year.
5. October comes after the month of _____.
6. December comes before the month of _____.
7. April comes between _____ and _____.
8. The middle two months of the year are _____ and _____.
9. There are _____ days in the month of January.
10. The month of June has _____ days.
11. November has exactly _____ days.
12. April, _____, _____ and _____ all contain 30 days.
13. Bonfire Night is November 5th. On this calendar it is a _____.
14. New Year's day is January 1st. On this calendar it is a _____.
15. The first day of the week is a _____.
16. The last day of the week is a _____.
17. There are _____ days in a week.
18. Monday comes between _____ and _____.
19. Saturday comes before _____.
20. On this calendar my birthday is on a _____.

CLOCKS

Clocks tell us the time.
This clock shows it is just after half past four.

Exercise 4

Match up the times shown in the table with the times shown on the clock faces.
The first one is done for you.

Time	Clock
Eleven o'clock	A
Half past six	
Half past eight	
Six o'clock	
Quarter to six	

Time	Clock
Three o'clock	
Half past three	
Quarter to three	
Quarter to twelve	
Half past ten	

Time	Clock
Ten o'clock	
Quarter to ten	
Quarter past one	
Quarter past six	
Twelve o'clock	

Clock A   Clock B   Clock C   Clock D   Clock E

Clock F   Clock G   Clock H   Clock J   Clock K

Clock L   Clock M   Clock N   Clock O   Clock P

TYPES OF CLOCKS

These clocks look different but they both tell the same time.
(Half past ten).

Analogue clocks
use hands

Digital clocks
use digits

Exercise 5

Match the times on the analogue and digital clocks with the times shown in the table.
The first one is done for you.

Time	Analogue	Digital
Quarter past one	1	h
Six o'clock		
Half past three		
Eight o'clock		
Nine o'clock		
Half past ten		
Two o'clock		
Quarter past six		
Quarter to one		
Quarter to three		

HOW LONG?

Barney's Day

Exercise 6

1. At what time does Barney ride to school?
2. When is Barney eating breakfast?
3. At what time is Barney watching television?
4. At what time is Barney cleaning his teeth?
5. At what time is Barney eating school lunch?
6. At what time is Barney asleep?
7. At what time is Barney in his Maths lesson?
8. When do we see Barney with his friends?
9. What is Barney doing at 7.45 in the evening?
10. What is Barney doing at 8.30 in the morning?

Exercise 7

Choose the right answer to each question

1. How long is it between Barney brushing his teeth and Barney eating his breakfast?
   a 2 hours   **b** 1 hour   **c** 15 minutes.
2. How long is it between Barney's Maths lesson and his eating lunch?
   a 3 hours   **b** 2 hours   **c** 2 hours 15 minutes.
3. How much time passes between Barney eating his breakfast and Barney cycling to school?
   a 1 hour   **b** 30 minutes   **c** 1 hour 30 minutes.
4. How much time passes between Barney's breakfast and his lunch?
   a 3 hours 30 minutes   **b** 4 hours   **c** 5 hours 15 minutes
5. How many hours pass between Barney's Maths lesson and his falling asleep?
   a 12 hours   **b** 10 hours   **c** No time

A.M. AND P.M.

9 o'clock happens twice a day:

9 o'clock in the morning

9 o'clock in the evening

9 o'clock in the morning is 9 a.m.

9 o'clock in the evening is 9 p.m.

You write a.m. for times before midday (noon)
and p.m. for times after midday.

Here are some things Barney does during one day.

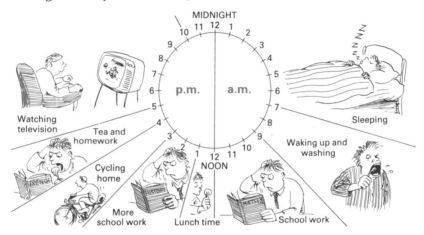

Exercise 8

Write a.m. or p.m. to make these sentences correct.

1. Barney is cycling home at 3 (a.m. or p.m.)
2. Barney is watching television at 8 (a.m. or p.m.)
3. Barney is cleaning his teeth at 7 (a.m. or p.m.)
4. Barney is fast asleep at 3 (a.m. or p.m.)
5. Barney is doing his work at 10 (a.m. or p.m.)
6. Barney finishes his lunch at 1 (a.m. or p.m.)
7. Barney starts homework and tea at 4 (a.m. or p.m.)
8. Barney goes to bed at 10 (a.m. or p.m.)
9. Barney starts his school day at 9 (a.m. or p.m.)
10. Barney starts his lunch break at 12 (noon or midnight)

ACTIVITY　Welcome to the Mad Hatter's Tea Party.

Everyone has a watch.
Each watch tells a different time.
Alice's watch tells the right time.

Remember:

The Dormouse's watch is two hours slow.
The Mad Hatter's watch is one hour fast.
The March Hare's watch is fifteen minutes fast.

Exercise 9

Fill in the table below. The first two lines have been done for you.

Alice's Watch	Dormouse's Watch	Mad Hatter's Watch	March Hare's Watch
10.00 a.m.	8.00 a.m.	11.00 a.m.	10.15 a.m.
9.30 a.m.	7.30 a.m.	10.30 a.m.	9.45 a.m.
6.00 a.m.			
8.00 a.m.			
7.30 a.m.			
11.30 a.m			
12.30 p.m.			
5.45 p.m.			
8.15 p.m.			
6.20 p.m.			
10.30 p.m.			
7.40 a.m.			
8.50 a.m.			
2.05 p.m.			
3.10 p.m.			

TIME LINES

Exercise 10

Here is a time line:

each gap
shows 1 year

1. Say which years are shown by these five pictures.

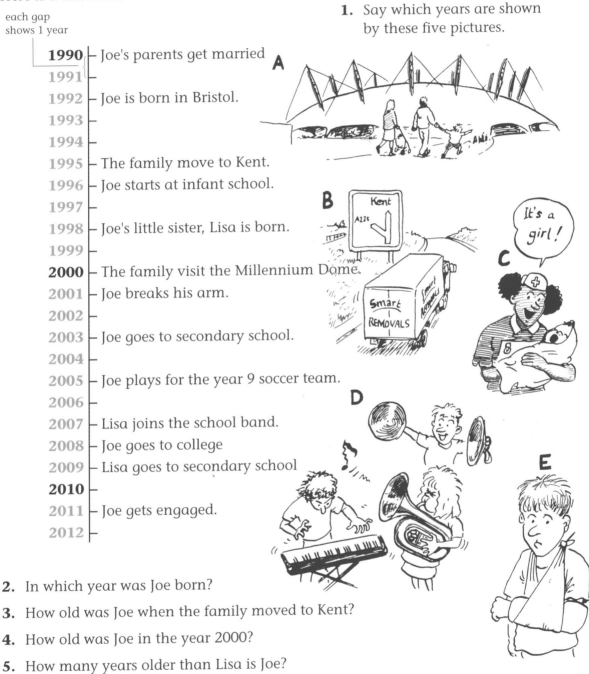

1990 – Joe's parents get married
1991 –
1992 – Joe is born in Bristol.
1993 –
1994 –
1995 – The family move to Kent.
1996 – Joe starts at infant school.
1997 –
1998 – Joe's little sister, Lisa is born.
1999 –
2000 – The family visit the Millennium Dome.
2001 – Joe breaks his arm.
2002 –
2003 – Joe goes to secondary school.
2004 –
2005 – Joe plays for the year 9 soccer team.
2006 –
2007 – Lisa joins the school band.
2008 – Joe goes to college
2009 – Lisa goes to secondary school
2010 –
2011 – Joe gets engaged.
2012 –

2. In which year was Joe born?

3. How old was Joe when the family moved to Kent?

4. How old was Joe in the year 2000?

5. How many years older than Lisa is Joe?

6. How old was Joe when he became engaged?

7. How many years are there between Joe starting infant school and him playing for the Year 9 team?

REVIEW 2

A. MENTAL ARITHMETIC

1. How many 5p coins are there in 25p?
2. What is 4 add 6, add 3 take away 7?
3. If you get 8 toffees in one box, how many will you get in 5 boxes?
4. How many days are there in three weeks?
5. What is 101 add 202?
6. How many 2p coins make 26p?
7. If James saves 50p a day, how much would he save in 9 days?
8. What is 12 add 11, add 6, take away 5?
9. If Mary spends 72p, how much change will she get from £1.00?
10. Add one to ninety-nine.

B. SHAPE

1. Name these shapes.

   a   **b**   **c**   **d**

2. Measure the radius of each circle.

   a   **b**   **c**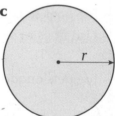

C. SYMMETRY

1. Match up the halves of these cars.

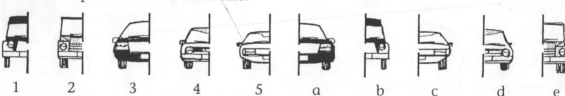

  1   2   3   4   5   a   b   c   d   e

2. Complete the mirror image to make four words.

   CODE   BOOK   HIDE   BOX

D. NUMBER WORK

Addition (×)

Addition workcard 1

1. $26 + 40 =$ 2. $30 + 50 =$
3. $40 + 30 =$ 4. $35 + 15 =$
5. $17 + 23 =$ 6. $30 + 60 =$
7. $21 + 39 =$ 8. $10 + 50 =$
9. $62 + 28 =$ 10. $14 + 26 =$
11. $33 + 27 =$ 12. $19 + 51 =$

Addition workcard 2

1. $5 + 27 =$ 2. $72 + 90 =$
3. $65 + 19 =$ 4. $37 + 36 =$
5. $38 + 4 =$ 6. $18 + 43 =$
7. $49 + 6 =$ 8. $7 + 25 =$
9. $55 + 8 =$ 10. $8 + 54 =$
11. $39 + 41 =$ 12. $74 + 6 =$

Subtraction (−)

Subtraction workcard 1

1. $9 - 6 =$ 2. $12 - 8 =$
3. $10 - 3 =$ 4. $15 - 9 =$
5. $17 - 8 =$ 6. $20 - 13 =$
7. $21 - 11 =$ 8. $23 - 17 =$
9. $22 - 15 =$ 10. $21 - 16 =$
11. $25 - 17 =$ 12. $26 - 19 =$

Subtraction workcard 2

1. $21 - 19 =$ 2. $33 - 26 =$
3. $24 - 15 =$ 4. $25 - 7 =$
5. $32 - 26 =$ 6. $37 - 28 =$
7. $25 - 10 =$ 8. $45 - 20 =$
9. $45 - 38 =$ 10. $26 - 10 =$
11. $34 - 10 =$ 12. $36 - 17 =$

Multiplication (×)

Tables workcard 1

1. $3 \times 4 =$ 2. $5 \times 3 =$ 3. $4 \times 2 =$ 4. $4 \times 5 =$ 5. $8 \times 2 =$
6. $3 \times 7 =$ 7. $6 \times 3 =$ 8. $5 \times 5 =$ 9. $3 \times 10 =$ 10. $10 \times 5 =$
11. $6 \times 6 =$ 12. $4 \times 8 =$ 13. $7 \times 10 =$ 14. $8 \times 5 =$ 15. $6 \times 7 =$

Division (÷)

Tables workcard 2

1. $6 \div 2 =$ 2. $8 \div 4 =$ 3. $6 \div 3 =$ 4. $10 \div 5 =$ 5. $8 \div 2 =$
6. $12 \div 2 =$ 7. $10 \div 2 =$ 8. $12 \div 4 =$ 9. $20 \div 5 =$ 10. $12 \div 3 =$
11. $20 \div 2 =$ 12. $24 \div 4 =$ 13. $20 \div 10 =$ 14. $24 \div 8 =$ 15. $30 \div 10 =$

E.   OPERATION SIGNS

Copy these and fill in the missing signs. Choose from +, −, ×, ÷.

1. 4 ☐ 2 = 6   **2.** 3 ☐ 3 = 9   **3.** 7 ☐ 4 = 11   **4.** 10 ☐ 4 = 6

5. 5 ☐ 5 = 25   **6.** 8 ☐ 2 = 4   **7.** 8 ☐ 1 = 7   **8.** 14 ☐ 4 = 18

9. 10 ☐ 2 = 5   **10.** 4 ☐ 4 = 16   **11.** 6 ☐ 9 = 15   **12.** 12 ☐ 12 = 0

F.   NUMBER PATTERNS

Fill in the missing numbers.

1. 2, 4, 6, ——, ——, 12   **2.** 4, 8, ——, 16, ——

3. 3, 6, ——, ——, 15   **4.** 3, 5, 7, ——, ——, ——

5. 7, 11, 15, ——, ——   **6.** 1, 6, 11, ——, ——

7. 9, ——, 17, 21, ——   **8.** 1, 7, 13, ——, ——

9. 2, 7, 12, ——, ——   **10.** 20, 18, 16, ——, ——

11. 18, 15, 12, ——, ——   **12.** 27, 25, ——, 21, ——

13. 31, 27, 23, ——, ——   **14.** 25, ——, 13, 7, ——

15. 23, 18, ——, 8, ——

G.   MONEY

48p   29p   37p   24p   26p

1. How much change from 50p would you get if you bought a cup of tea?

2. How much change from 50p would you get if you bought a bar of chocolate?

3. How much change from 50p would you get if you bought a bottle of pop?

4. How much change from 50p would you get if you bought a comic?

5. How much change from 50p would you get if you bought a cake?

6. How much would cake and a cup of tea cost together?

7. How much would a comic and a bar of chocolate cost?

8. How much would a bottle of pop and a comic cost?

9. How much would a comic and a cake cost?

10. How much would a cup of tea and a bar of chocolate cost?

H. DECIMALS

1. What decimal part of each shape is shaded?

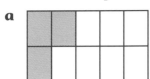 **a**   **b** 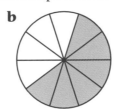   **c**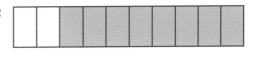

2. Match each drawing with a decimal from the box.

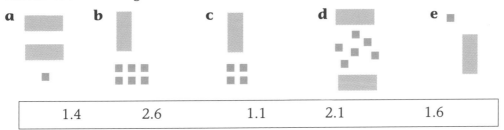

| 1.4 | 2.6 | 1.1 | 2.1 | 1.6 |

3. Fill in the missing decimals on this scale.

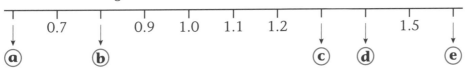

I. TIME

1. Match the written time with the correct clock time.

a    **b**   **c**   **d** 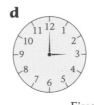   **e**

Three o'clock   Half past nine   Five o'clock

Quarter to ten   Ten past five

2. If it is now 5 o'clock, what time will it be in five hours?

3. Does this clock show a quarter past or a quarter to five?   `4:45`

4. If it is now half past two, what time will it be in five hours?

5. Does this clock show a quarter past or a quarter to six?   `6:15`

6. If it is now 8 o'clock, what will the time be in $2\frac{1}{2}$ hours?

(11) RELATIONS

This unit will help you to:
→ **understand a family tree**
→ **compare heights and lengths**
→ **use the symbols >, <.**

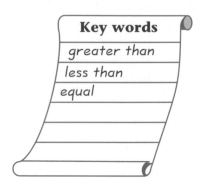

Key words

greater than

less than

equal

FAMILY TREE

This is the Morris Family Tree

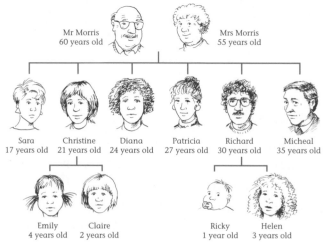

Mr Morris
60 years old

Mrs Morris
55 years old

Sara
17 years old

Christine
21 years old

Diana
24 years old

Patricia
27 years old

Richard
30 years old

Micheal
35 years old

Emily
4 years old

Claire
2 years old

Ricky
1 year old

Helen
3 years old

Exercise 1

Copy and complete the sentences.

1. Helen is —— years old.

2. Sara is —— years old.

3. Mr Morris is —— years old.

4. Ricky is —— year old.

5. Mr and Mrs Morris have —— children.

6. Mr and Mrs Morris have —— grandchildren.

7. Altogether there are —— people in the family

Exercise 2

Answer these questions.

1. Who is the mother of Emily and Claire?

2. Who is Helen's father?

3. What is the name of Richard's brother?

4. How much older is Mr Morris than his wife?

5. Who is the younger, Emily or Ricky?

6. How many children has Richard?

7. Who is Claire's sister?

Taller or Shorter?

In the picture Don is **shorter than** Pat. Adam is **taller than** Don. Paul's legs are **longer than** Don's.

Pat   Don   Adam   Paul   Linda   Roy   Janet

Exercise 3

In the picture above:

1. Who is the tallest person?
2. Who is the shortest person?
3. Who is taller, Pat or Linda?
4. Is Don taller than Linda?
5. Who is taller than Roy?
6. What is the name of the shortest girl?
7. Who is about half as tall as Paul?
8. Who do you think is the heaviest?
9. How many people are taller than Pat?
10. Who is taller than Pat but shorter than Adam?

Exercise 4

Measure these lines carefully. Use all the measurements to answer the questions below.

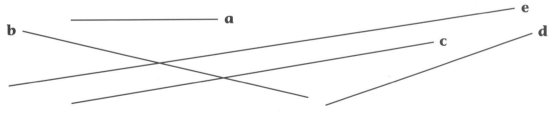

1. Line **a** = ____ cm,   Line **b** = ____ cm,   Line **c** = ____ cm,   Line **d** = ____ cm, Line **e** = ____ cm.
2. Which line is 2 cm shorter than line **c**?
3. Line **b** is ____ cm longer than line **d**.
4. The difference between line **d** and line **a** is ____ cm.
5. Which line is half the length of line **b**?
6. Which pair of lines joined end-to-end, are 4 cm longer than line **e**?
7. Which two lines joined end-to-end, are exactly the same length as line **c**?
8. Which pairs of lines joined end-to-end, are the same length as line **e**?

MORE OR LESS?

These scales do not balance:

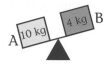

You can say that A weighs **more than** B.
            or B weighs **less than** A.

Example 1

a Which weighs more?
b How much more?

    a   A weighs more
    b   A weighs 8 kg more than B.

Exercise 5

1. Copy and complete the sentences below using one of the expressions:

       'weighs more than'   'weighs less than'   'weighs the same as'

The first one has been done for you.

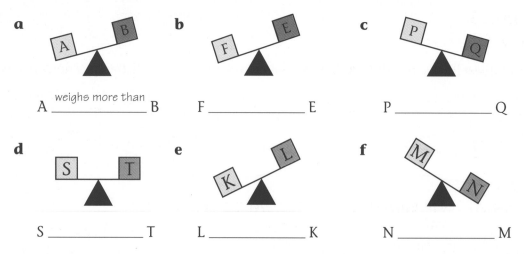

A <u>weighs more than</u> B   F _____ E   P _____ Q

S _____ T   L _____ K   N _____ M

2. Which weighs more? How much more?

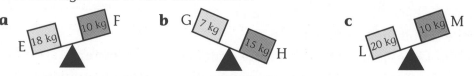

d   In which drawing is one of the weights twice (×2) as heavy as the other.

NUMERACY EQUAL OR NOT?

Sometimes scales balance:

Sometimes they don't

A weighs the same as B
You can say A = B
A = B means A is the same as B.

G weighs more than H
You say G ≠ H
G ≠ H means G is not the same as H.

Exercise 6

Use the sign '=' for 'the same as' and use the sign '≠' for 'not the same as'.
The first one is done for you.

1.

A ≠ B

2.

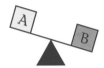

3.

4.

5.

6.

Example 2

Replace the ☐ with = or ≠:

a $2 + 3 \ \square \ 6 - 1$ **b** $9 + 7 \ \square \ 13 - 3$

a $2 + 3 = 5$ ⎫
⎬ the answers
$6 - 1 = 5$ ⎭ are the same

so $2 + 3 = 6 - 1$.

b $9 + 7 = 16$ ⎫
⎬ the answers are
$13 - 3 = 10$ ⎭ not the same

so $9 + 7 \neq 13 - 3$

Exercise 7

Replace the ☐ with the '=' sign or the '≠' sign in these sums.

1. $2 + 1 \ \square \ 4 - 1$
2. $5 + 3 \ \square \ 3 + 1$
3. $7 + 3 \ \square \ 5 + 5$

4. $10 + 2 \ \square \ 11 + 3$
5. $15 + 1 \ \square \ 17 - 3$
6. $2 + 8 + 6 \ \square \ 8 + 8$

7. $29 - 2 \ \square \ 8 + 8 + 8$
8. $9 + 2 + 10 \ \square \ 11 + 12$
9. $17 - 17 \ \square \ 12 - 3 - 9$

10. $18 + 3 \ \square \ 13 + 8 + 1$
11. $5 + 4 \ \square \ 13 - 4$
12. $27 - 3 - 2 \ \square \ 11 + 11$

13. $19 - 18 \ \square \ 26 - 25$
14. $9 + 15 \ \square \ 30 - 6$
15. $14 + 17 \ \square \ 6 + 21$

16. $28 - 9 \ \square \ 6 + 9 + 4$
17. $15 + 15 \ \square \ 15 - 15$
18. $22 + 0 \ \square \ 22 - 0$

19. $6 + 22 \ \square \ 30 - 2$
20. $7 - 3 \ \square \ 49 - 6 - 20$

USING SYMBOLS

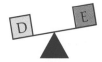

D weighs more than E
You can write D > E
This means D is more than E.

P weighs less than Q
You can write P < Q
This means P is less than Q.

Exercise 8

Use the sign '>' for 'more than' or '<' to mean 'less than'.
The first one is done for you.

1.

A > B

2.

A ..... B

3.

C ..... D

4.

X ..... Y

5.

F ..... G

6.

G ..... F

Example 3

Use > or < in place of □:

a   3 □ 4   **b**   52 □ 19

a   3 is less than 4

so 3 < 4.

b   52 is more than 19

so 52 > 19

Exercise 9

Replace the □ with '>' or '<'.

1. 6 □ 4
2. 10 □ 2
3. 13 □ 11
4. 5 □ 11
5. 21 □ 15
6. 16 □ 25
7. 33 □ 60
8. 64 □ 72
9. 87 □ 17
10. 71 □ 68
11. 101 □ 99
12. 201 □ 199
13. 167 □ 200
14. 267 □ 266
15. 461 □ 497

Exercise 10

Use the > sign or the < sign in the questions below.

1. 6 + 2 ☐ 9   **2.** 7 + 2 ☐ 8   **3.** 7 + 3 ☐ 11

4. 5 ☐ 6 − 2   **5.** 6 + 4 ☐ 7   **6.** 7 + 4 ☐ 12

7. 13 ☐ 6 − 1   **8.** 15 ☐ 12 + 5   **9.** 16 ☐ 20 − 3

10. 16 − 3 ☐ 12 − 1   **11.** 17 + 4 ☐ 13 + 5   **12.** 19 + 2 ☐ 18 + 4

13. 20 + 4 ☐ 16 + 6   **14.** 21 − 2 ☐ 17 + 1   **15.** 22 + 6 ☐ 5 + 24

16. 18 + 9 ☐ 20 + 5   **17.** 31 − 2 ☐ 24 + 3   **18.** 35 + 1 ☐ 38 − 3

19. 40 − 7 ☐ 31 + 5   **20.** 43 − 10 ☐ 29 + 5

How many times more?

Aran has 3 sweets in his hand,
Nita has 6 sweets in hers.

You can say that Nita has **two times** more sweets.

Rui has 3 sweets in his hand,
Elizabeth 9 sweets in hers.

You can say that Elizabeth has **three times** more sweets.

Exercise 11

Who has more sweets? How many times more?

1. Anna   Bharaj   2. Catie   Delroy   3. Eli   Frank

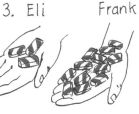

4. Gita   Helen   5. Ian   Jenny   6. Kuldip   Lurch

12 FAIR SHARES

Key words

exactly
half
quarter
divide

This unit will help you to:
→ **understand fair shares**
→ **find half and a quarter of an amount**
→ **recognise $\frac{1}{2}$s and $\frac{1}{4}$s.**

IT'S NOT FAIR!

Liz is the unfairest girl in the world.
This exercise shows you why.

IT'S JUST NOT FAIR!

Exercise 1

1. Liz pours some cola for herself
   and her brother, James.

   Has Liz shared the cola fairly?

2. James complains to Mum because
   he has not got a full glass of cola.
   So Liz gets another glass and fills it up.

   Has James got a fair share of the cola?

3. Liz is having tea with two friends.
   The cake should be cut into three
   equal pieces.

   a Has the cake been cut into three
   equal pieces?

   b Has the cake been shared fairly?

4. Liz has to cut these cakes and pies into equal pieces.
   Have they been cut into equal pieces or into unequal pieces?

 a    **b**   **c**

Exercise 2

1. Liz shares sweets with James. The sweets should be shared equally.

    a Has Liz shared the sweets fairly?

    b How much should each one have?

2. Liz is sharing £10 with her brother.

    a How many coins should each have?

    b How many more coins does Liz have to give James so that he has half?

3. Liz is sharing 9 cakes with two friends.

    a How many cakes should each get when they are shared fairly?

    b If there were 12 cakes, how many should each get?

4. Liz was told that she could eat half of the chocolates in this box.

    a Has Liz eaten her fair share?

    b How many chocolates **should** she have eaten?

5. The buttons have been shared into groups, but Liz has done it unfairly. How many buttons should be in each group?

a

b

c

HALF AND $\frac{1}{2}$

Liz has to pick up half of the cards.
There were 8 cards so Liz has taken 4 cards.

To find a half of an amount you divide it into 2 equal groups. In digits a half is $\frac{1}{2}$.

Exercise 3

1. Check that Liz has picked up exactly half of the cards.

Write   'exactly $\frac{1}{2}$'   'more than $\frac{1}{2}$'   or   'less than $\frac{1}{2}$'

a

b

c

d

e

f

2. In this question Liz has already taken half of the cards.
Work out how many cards there were to start with.

a

b

c

d

e

f

MAKING QUARTERS

Here are **8** counters. They can be arranged in **4 equal** groups.

Each group is a quarter.

 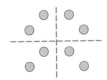

To find a quarter of an amount you divide it into 4 equal groups.
In digits a quarter is $\frac{1}{4}$.

Here are another 8 counters.

They are divided into **4** groups, but **they are not quarters**, because the groups are not equal.

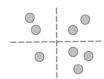

Exercise 4

1. Only one of the drawings shows quarters.
   Which drawing is it?

a   **b**   **c**   **d**

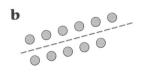 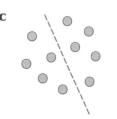 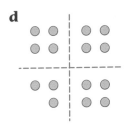

e   **f**   **g**   **h**

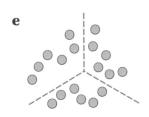 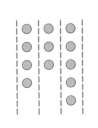 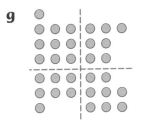 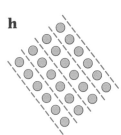

2. Which of the drawings shows the group divided into halves?

3. Make a drawing to show 20 counters divided into $\frac{1}{4}$s.

Exercise 5

Copy and complete these sentences.
The pictures will help you.

1. $\frac{1}{2}$ of 18 is _____

2. $\frac{1}{4}$ of 16 is _____

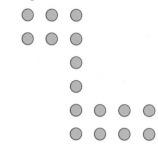

3. $\frac{1}{4}$ of 24 is _____

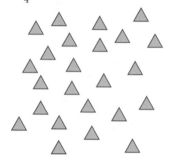

4. $\frac{1}{2}$ of 16 is _____

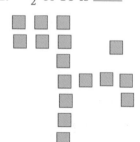

5. $\frac{1}{4}$ of 12 is _____

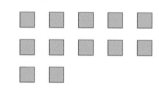

6. $\frac{1}{4}$ of 4 is _____

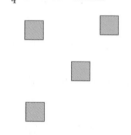

HALVES AND QUARTERS OF SHAPES

This shape shows halves:

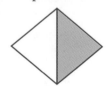

One half, $\frac{1}{2}$, is shaded.

This shape shows quarters:

One quarter, $\frac{1}{4}$, is shaded.

Exercise 6

Write down what fraction is shaded.
Write ' $\frac{1}{2}$ ' or ' $\frac{1}{4}$ '.

1.

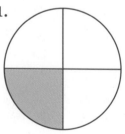

2.

3.

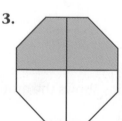

4.

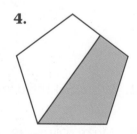

13 CODES

This unit will help you to:
→ **use codes**
→ **use letters to stand for numbers**
→ **substitute numbers into simple expressions**
→ **solve simple equations by balancing.**

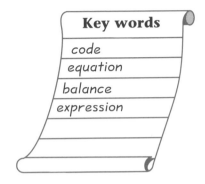

Key words

code
equation
balance
expression

USING CODES

Exercise 1

In this simple code each number stands for a letter:

A	C	E	H	I	S	T
1	2	3	4	5	6	7

Use the code to find out what these messages mean.

1. 6,3,3   7,4,3   2,1,7

2. 4,3   5,6   1   2,4,3,1,7

3. 7,4,1,7   5,6   4,5,6   2,1,7

4. 5   4,1,7,3   7,4,1,7   4,1,7

5. 7,1,6,7,3   7,4,3   7,3,1

Exercise 2

Here is a map of enemy territory.
Use the code to work out what is at each place on the map.

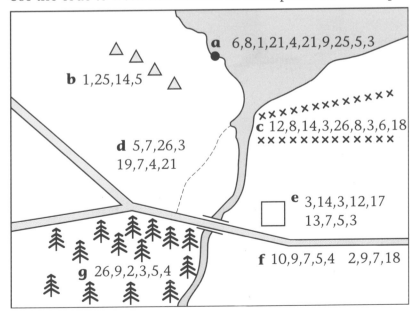

Code

1	G	14	N
2	R	15	V
3	E	16	J
4	T	17	Y
5	S	18	D
6	L	19	P
7	A	20	X
8	I	21	H
9	O	22	W
10	C	23	Q
11	Z	24	K
12	M	25	U
13	B	26	F

a 6,8,1,21,4,21,9,25,5,3

b 1,25,14,5

c 12,8,14,3,26,8,3,6,18

d 5,7,26,3
19,7,4,21

e 3,14,3,12,17
13,7,5,3

f 10,9,7,5,4   2,9,7,18

g 26,9,2,3,5,4

Exercise 3

One of these people is a spy.

De-code the clues and find which one is the spy.

The code												
A	B	C	D	E	F	G	H	I	J	K	L	M
6	19	14	3	17	13	5	16	8	22	15	1	7
N	O	P	Q	R	S	T	U	V	W	X	Y	Z
11	12	4	18	10	25	9	23	21	2	24	20	26

Jim   Bob   Tom   Boris   Harry   James   Jon   Emma

Clue 1.

Message number one

16, 17   16, 6, 25   11, 12   19, 17, 6, 10, 3

Clue 2.

Message number two

9, 16, 17   25, 4, 20   2, 17, 6, 10, 25   5, 1, 6, 25, 25, 17, 25

Clue 3.

Message number three

16, 17   8, 25   9, 6, 1, 1   19, 23, 9   11, 12, 9   9, 16, 17   9, 6, 1, 1, 17, 25, 9

Who is the spy?

Exercise 4

Here is a code:

A	B	C	D	E	F	G	H	I
20	6	11	16	22	30	8	17	5

	J	K	L	M	N	O	P	Q	
	46	34	12	27	15	9	14	24	

R	S	T	U	V	W	X	Y	Z
40	7	13	4	2	23	29	10	19

1. De-code this message to find out how Bill got his black eye.
   Each line is a new word.

   $(14 + 3), (11 + 11)$

   $(19 - 8), (34 - 14), (24 - 12), (32 - 20), (26 - 4), (21 - 5)$

   $(12 \div 2), (20 \div 4), (24 \div 3)$

   $(6 \times 5), (5 \times 8), (2 \times 11), (4 \times 4)$

   $(1 + 19)$

   $(14 - 7), (25 - 11), (26 - 17), (14 - 1), (20 - 7), (40 - 30)$

   $(4 \times 3), (3 + 17), (31 - 21), (4 \times 5), (18 \div 3), (11 - 2), (12 \div 3), (2 + 11)$

2. Using the same code, find out what the bear is thinking to himself.

13,17,22 ~ 6,22,20,40 ~
8,9,22,7 ~
17,4,15,13,5,15,8.

40,22,20,16,10 ~ 13,9 ~
12,22,20,14 ~ 9,15 ~
17,5,7 ~ 14,40,22,10.

23,17,20,13 ~
13,40,22,20,13 ~
13,9,15,5,8,17,13?

Exercise 5

Answer these questions about yourself. Put your answers into code using the code at the top of the page.

1. What is your first name?

2. What is your favourite colour?

3. Which pop group or singer do you like?

FRED'S CAFÉ

When Fred is taking an order he uses a short-hand code.
If you order 'A glass of kola and a sandwich' he will write: $k + s$
You can see Fred's code written on the menu.

Exercise 6

Write these orders in Fred's code.
The first one is done for you.

1. The cost of a cup of tea and a sandwich = $t + s$.

2. The cost of a cup of tea and a cake.

3. The cost of a glass of kola and a bun.

4. The cost of a bun and a sandwich.

5. The cost of a cup of tea and a glass of kola.

Exercise 7

Use Fred's menu to work out the amount of each bill.
The first one is done for you.

1. $t + c = 40 + 30 = 70$ pence
2. $t + k =$
3. $b + c =$
4. $b + t =$
5. $f + c =$
6. $s + f =$
7. $t + s =$
8. $f + b + s =$
9. $c + s + t =$
10. $s + s + t + k =$

Exercise 8

Here are six more orders. Write them using Fred's code.
The first one is done for you.

1. 2 teas = $2t$
2. 3 cakes
3. 2 kolas
4. 4 teas
5. 3 sandwiches
6. 2 teas and a bun

NUMERACY

When you pay for your order, Fred uses the menu to find the value of each symbol.

If the order was *f* + *c*, (a fizzpop and a cake), he sees that:

f is 50p and *c* is 30p.

So the total bill is 50p + 30p = 80p

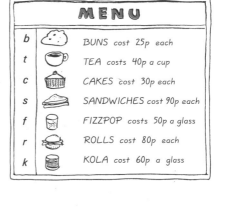

MENU

b		BUNS cost 25p each
t		TEA costs 40p a cup
c		CAKES cost 30p each
s		SANDWICHES cost 90p each
f		FIZZPOP costs 50p a glass
r		ROLLS cost 80p each
k		KOLA cost 60p a glass

Exercise 9

Use the menu to work out Fred's bill.

ORDER 1
$c + k =$
30 + 60 = 90p
Paid

ORDER 2
$t + b =$

ORDER 3
$r + s =$

ORDER 4
$k + r =$

ORDER 5
$2t =$
2 teas
= 2 × 40
= 80p *Paid*

ORDER 6
$3c =$

ORDER 7
$2f =$

ORDER 8
$4t =$

ORDER 9
$s + k =$

ORDER 10
$2t + b =$

ORDER 11
$2k + c =$

ORDER 12
$f + 2r =$

Exercise 10

Find the value of these expressions if:

$v = 2$ $w = 5$ $x = 1$ $y = 9$ and $z = 11$.

The first one is done for you.

1. $x + y = 1 + 9 = 10$
2. $v + z$
3. $z + x$
4. $y + v$
5. $y + w$
6. $v + x + y$
7. $x + z + y$
8. $w + x + y$
9. $x + v + w$
10. $x + v + v$

SIMPLE EQUATIONS

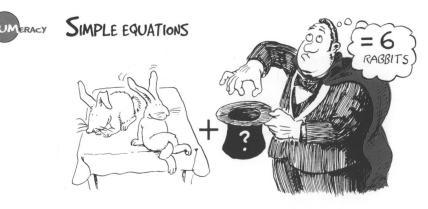

The Great Magico knows that he has 6 rabbits altogether.
He takes 2 rabbits from the hat. How many rabbits are left in the hat?

$$2 + \square = 6$$

so, $\square = 4$

Exercise 11

Work out the missing number:

1. $4 + \square = 6$ **2.** $2 + \square = 6$ **3.** $5 + \square = 9$

4. $3 + \square = 7$ **5.** $5 + \square = 11$ **6.** $9 + \square = 11$

7. $7 + \square = 9$ **8.** $5 + \square = 15$ **9.** $9 + \square = 14$

10. $10 + \square = 20$ **11.** $20 + \square = 25$ **12.** $\square + 4 = 16$

13. $\square + 3 = 6$ **14.** $\square + 1 = 6$ **15.** $\square + 11 = 13$

Magico puts five
bottles in a box,
and closes the lid.

When he opens the
box there is only
one bottle left.

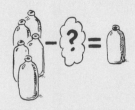

How many bottles
has Magico made
disappear?

Exercise 12

Find the missing numbers:

1. $6 - \square = 4$ **2.** $7 - \square = 4$ **3.** $9 - \square = 7$ **4.** $8 - \square = 5$

5. $10 - \square = 4$ **6.** $13 - \square = 7$ **7.** $18 - \square = 9$ **8.** $20 - \square = 15$

9. $30 - \square = 21$ **10.** $35 - \square = 29$ **11.** $50 - \square = 30$ **12.** $50 - \square = 32$

BALANCING

These scales do not balance:

a is lighter, than *b*.

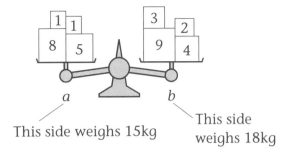

This side weighs 15kg

This side weighs 18kg

Exercise 13

Do these scales balance?
If not which side is lighter?

1.

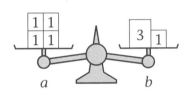

2.

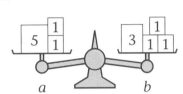

3.

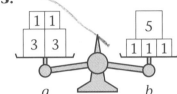

4.

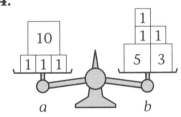

5.

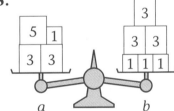

6.

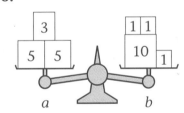

7.

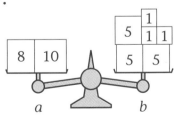

8.

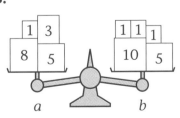

9.

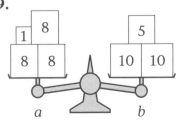

You can make scales balance by adding weights to the lighter side.

To balance these scales, the missing weight must be 3 kg:

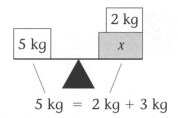

5 kg = 2 kg + 3 kg

Exercise 14

Find the missing weights to make the scales balance:

1.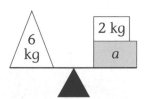

2.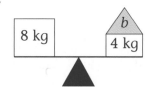

3.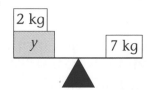

4.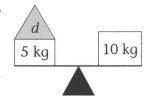

5.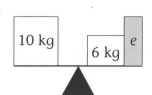

6.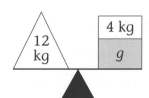

7.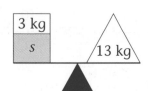

8.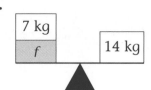

9.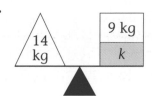

10.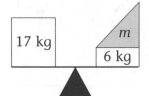

11.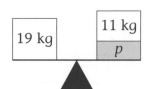

12.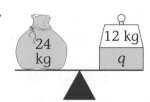

13.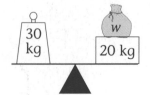

14.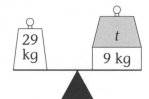

15.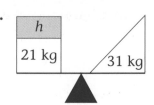

14 LENGTH

Key words

accurate

perimeter

distance
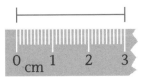

This unit will help you to:
→ **measure lines accurately using a ruler**
→ **find the perimeter of shapes**
→ **find missing lengths.**

MEASURING LINES

Exercise 1

Measure these lines to the nearest half ($\frac{1}{2}$) centimetre.
Remember to measure from the zero mark on your ruler.

1. ▬▬▬▬▬▬

2. ▬▬▬▬▬▬▬▬▬▬▬▬▬▬

3. ▬▬▬▬▬▬▬▬▬▬

4. ▬▬▬▬▬▬▬▬▬▬▬▬

5. ▬▬▬▬▬▬▬

6. ▬▬▬▬▬▬▬▬▬▬▬

Exercise 2

Measure the distance around the top of these boxes by measuring the length of each side then adding the distances together.

1 **a** Length A to B = _____ cm

    b Length B to C = _____ cm

    c Length C to D = _____ cm

    d Length D to A = _____ cm

    e Distance all the way round = _____ cm

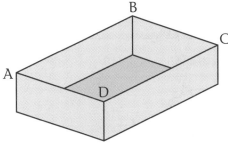

2 **a** Length A to B = _____ cm

    b Length B to C = _____ cm

    c Length C to A = _____ cm

    d Distance all the way round = _____ cm

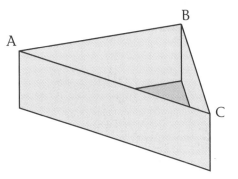

PERIMETER

The **total distance** around a shape is called the **perimeter**.

Exercise 3

Measure these shapes. Work out the perimeter of each.

1.

Perimeter = _____ cm

2.

Perimeter = _____ cm

3.

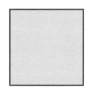

Perimeter = _____ cm

4.

Perimeter = _____ cm

5.

Perimeter = _____ cm

6.

Perimeter = _____ cm

7.

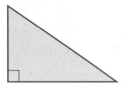

Perimeter = _____ cm

8.

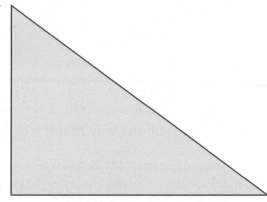

Perimeter = _____ cm

ADDING UP

To find the perimeter of a shape you add up
the lengths of all the sides.

Example 1

To find the perimeter of a rectangle,
add the sides together.
Like this:

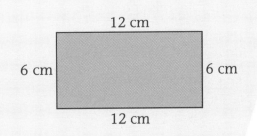

12 cm + 12 cm + 6 cm + 6 cm = 36 cm
The perimeter of this rectangle is 36 cm.

Exercise 4

Find the perimeter of these shapes.
These drawings are not full size.

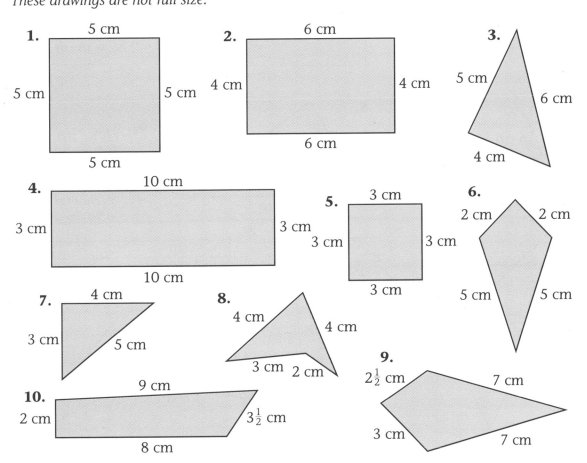

 FINDING MISSING SIDES

Example 2

Look at the rectangle below. Its perimeter is 24 cm.
Try to find the missing length.

The three sides you know
add up to: 8 + 4 + 8 = 20 cm

The perimeter is 24 cm.
So the missing side is 4 cm.

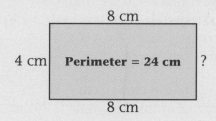

Exercise 5

Find the missing length in each drawing.
These drawings are not full size.

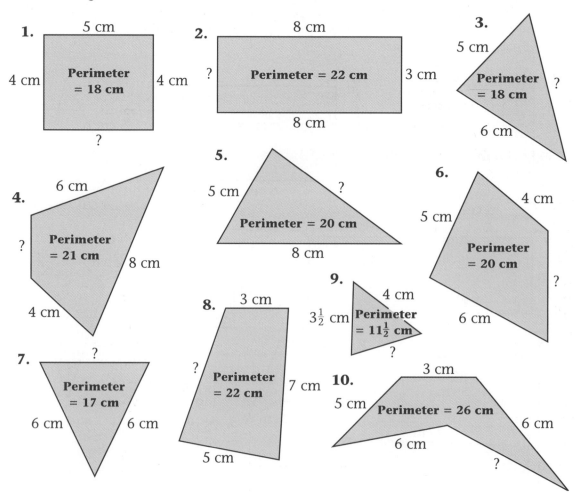

15 ANGLES

This unit will help you to:
→ **recognise right angles**
→ **use the terms acute, obtuse, reflex, right angle**
→ **estimate the size of an angle in degrees**
→ **use a protractor to measure angles**
→ **use a protractor to draw angles.**

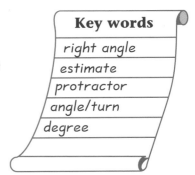

Key words

| right angle |
| estimate |
| protractor |
| angle/turn |
| degree |

RIGHT ANGLES

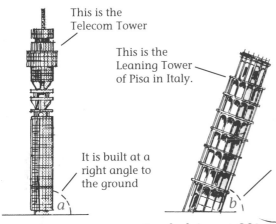

This is the Telecom Tower

This is the Leaning Tower of Pisa in Italy.

It is built at a right angle to the ground

Angle *a* is 90°

It was built at a right angle to the ground but over the years it has sunk on one side. Now it is **not** at a right angle.

Angle *b* is not 90°

The **right angle** is a very important angle.
We use **right angles** to construct most of our buildings. The corners of your table, your books and the windows in your room are right angles.

Exercise 1

Judge which of the angles below are **right angles**.

1.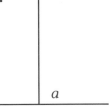
a

2.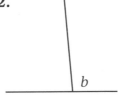
b

3.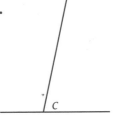
c

4.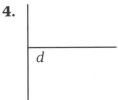
d

5.
e

6.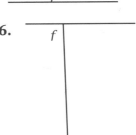
f

Example 1

The legs of the chair are at right angles to the floor.
The right angles are labelled with the letter '*r*'.

The back of the chair is not at right angles to the seat.
The angle is bigger than a right angle. It is lettered '*n*'.

Exercise 2

Say which of the lettered angles below are at right angles.

Exercise 3

Draw these lines at full size in your book.
The drawings are not shown full size.

1. 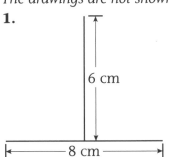   **2.** 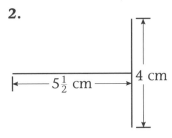   **3.**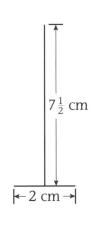

Exercise 4

Look at these angles. Decide if each angle is a right angle, bigger than a right angle or smaller than a right angle.

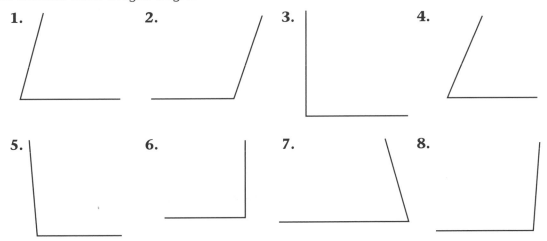

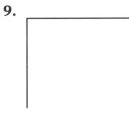

Copy out this table and put the number of each angle in the correct column.

Bigger than a right angle	Right angle	Smaller than a right angle

TYPES OF ANGLES

Watch what happens as the girl turns one arm of the fan.

The angle between the arms gets bigger.
The angle is the amount of turn between the two arms.

Here are five drawings showing the fan unfolding.
Under each drawing is a name. The name tells you what type of angle is shown by the fan.

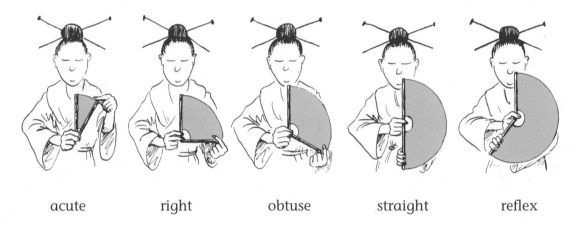

acute   right   obtuse   straight   reflex

Here are some more examples of angles.

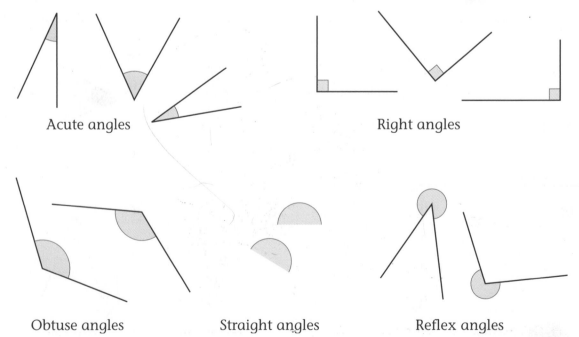

Acute angles   Right angles

Obtuse angles   Straight angles   Reflex angles

Exercise 5

Name these angles.
Write 'acute' 'obtuse' 'right angle' 'straight angle' or 'reflex'.

1.

acute

2.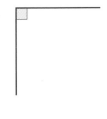

_____

3.

_____

4.

_____

5.

_____

6.

_____

7.

_____

8.

_____

9.

_____

10.

_____

11.

_____

12.

_____

13.

_____

14.

_____

15.

_____

16.

_____

17.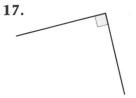

_____

18.

_____

19.

_____

20.

_____

DEGREES

An angle is a measure of turn.

You measure an angle in degrees, ° for short.

A full turn
is 360 degrees

A half turn
is 180 degrees

A quarter turn,
or right angle
is 90 degrees

360°

180°

90°

You can use a right angle, 90°, to estimate other angles.

Example 2

The arms on the girl's fan have turned **less than a right angle**, so you know that the angle between the arms is **less than 90°**.

Exercise 6

Look at the angles between the arms of these fans. Imagine that you were measuring them. Think of the right angle and decide which of the two measurements could be correct.

1.

70° or 140°

2.

30° or 150°

3.

10° or 170°

4.

60° or 120°

USING A PROTRACTOR

A protractor is used to measure angles. It has two scales.
Both scales start at zero and finish at 180°.

Example 3

Find the angle shown
on this protractor.

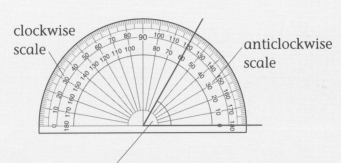

clockwise scale

anticlockwise scale

This angle is either 60° or 120°.

To work out which it is, you compare the angle with a right angle, 90°.
It is **smaller** than 90°.
So it is 60°.

Exercise 7

Decide whether the angles are bigger or smaller than 90°.
Use the protractors to measure the size of each angle.

1.

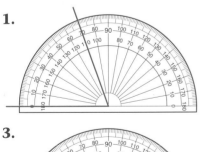

2.

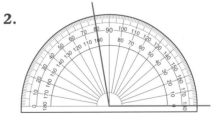

3.

4.

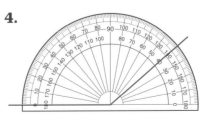

5.

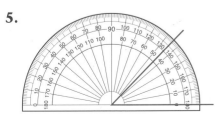

6.

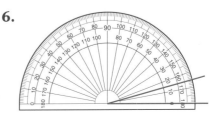

Exercise 8

Measure these angles.
Place your protractor carefully.

1.

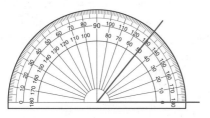

2.

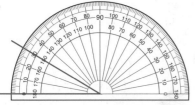

3.

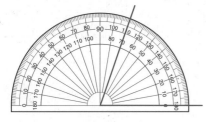

4.

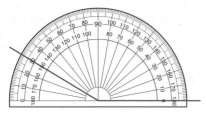

5.

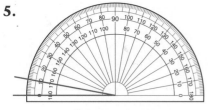

6.

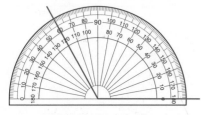

7.

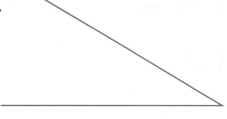

8.

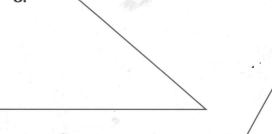

9.

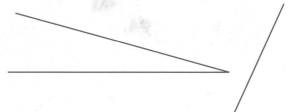

10.

11.

12.

DRAWING ANGLES

Drawing an angle of 60°

If you are left-handed, you will find it easier to draw the angle in this direction.

———————	**a** Draw a line about 6 cm long.	———————
	b Place the centre of the protractor at one end of the line.	
	c Find the 60° mark on the correct scale. Carefully mark the paper.	
60°	**d** Now join this mark to the end of the line.	60°

Exercise 9

Draw these angles in your book, using a protractor.

1. 30°	**2.** 50°	**3.** 70°	**4.** 90°
5. 100°	**6.** 130°	**7.** 45°	**8.** 35°
9. 65°	**10.** 125°	**11.** 145°	**12.** 105°
13. 15°	**14.** 115°	**15.** 10°	**16.** 135°

16 HANDLING DATA

This unit will help you to:
→ **use tally marks**
→ **make frequency tables**
→ **read pictograms and bar charts**
→ **draw pictograms and bar charts**
→ **find the mode from a bar chart.**

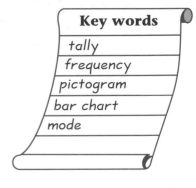

Key words
tally
frequency
pictogram
bar chart
mode

TALLY CHARTS AND PICTOGRAMS

When you count a group of items, it is useful to keep a 'tally'.
For each item in the group, you make one mark.
Each group of 5 is shown like this: ⑷. This makes the marks easier to count.

Here are 3 dots •• As you count each one you mark. ||| = 3.

Here are 5 dots •••• This is shown as ⑷ = 5

Here are 9 dots •••• This is shown as ⑷ |||| = 9

Exercise 1

What numbers are shown here?

1. |||| = 4

2. ⑷ =

3. ⑷ || =

4. ⑷ ⑷ =

5. ⑷ ⑷ ||| =

6. ⑷ ⑷ ⑷ =

7. ⑷ ⑷ ⑷ ⑷ =

8. ⑷ ⑷ ⑷ |||| =

9. ⑷ ⑷ | =

10. ⑷ ⑷ |||| =

11. ⑷ ⑷ ⑷ ||| =

12. ⑷ | =

13. ⑷ ||| =

14. ⑷ ⑷ ⑷ ⑷ |||| =

15. ⑷ ⑷ ⑷ || =

Exercise 2

Write these numbers using tally marks.

1. 14 = ⑷ ⑷ ||||

2. 7

3. 12

4. 16

5. 14

6. 17

7. 20

8. 22

9. 15

10. 23

11. 19

12. 13

13. 25

14. 27

15. 31

Exercise 3

Here are a group of shapes.

Copy the tally chart below. As you count each type of shape, make a mark on the chart. The circles have been counted for you.

Shape	Tally	Frequency
●	𝍤 ‖	7
■		
▲		
▬		

Frequency means total

Exercise 4

From the tally chart in Exercise 3 we can make a display.
Here is the completed tally chart, and a pictogram displaying the information.

Shape	Tally	Frequency
●	𝍤 ‖	7
■	𝍤 𝍤	10
▲	𝍤 ‖	7
▬	𝍤	5

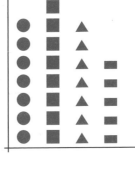

1. How many circles are there?
2. How many squares are there?
3. How many triangles are there?
4. How many rectangles are there?
5. How many shapes are there in all?

Exercise 5

Copy the tally chart and pictogram and complete both for this group of shapes.

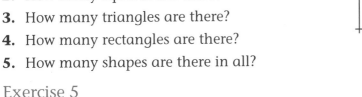

Shape	Tally	Frequency
◆	‖‖	3
●		
▲		
■		

Exercise 6

Here are the maths grades given to class 7B.

B	—	C	—	B	—	C	—	D	—	E	—	C	—	C	—	C
A	—	D	—	F	—	B	—	C	—	D	—	B	—	C	—	A
E	—	B	—	C	—	E	—	C	—	D	—	F	—	A	—	C

1. Complete the tally chart.
2. Complete the pictogram.

Grade	Tally	Frequency
A	|||	3
B		
C		
D		
E		
F		

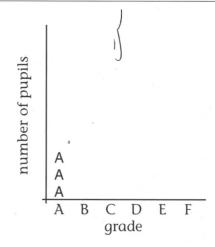

Exercise 7

People walking past the school gate were asked their favourite colour.
Here are the results.

Red	Blue	Red	Yellow	Blue	Green	Red	Green	Brown
Green	Red	Blue	Pink	Yellow	Blue	Blue	Blue	Green	Red
Blue	Brown	Yellow	Green	Blue	Red	Blue	Brown	Blue

1. Complete the tally chart.
2. Complete the pictogram.

Colour	Tally	Frequency
Red	|||||		6
Blue		
Yellow		
Green		
Brown		
Pink		

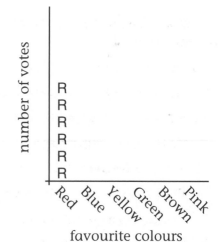

favourite colours

3. Which is the most popular colour?
4. Which colour got least votes?
5. Which colours got the same number of votes?
6. Which colour got five votes?
7. How many people voted?

Exercise 8

Here are five items that are sold in the school tuck shop.

Cola

Crisps

Toffees

Chocolate

Chews

The pictogram shows how many of each item were sold during break time.

1. How many packs of toffees were sold?

2. How many bottles of cola were sold?

3. How many bags of crisps were sold?

4. How many bars of chocolate were sold?

5. Which item sold most?

6. Which item sold least?

7. Which two items sold the same amount?

8. How many items were sold in all?

number of items sold

tuck shop items

Exercise 9

When a class voted for their favourite sweets, this was the result.

Lolly pop

Ice cream

Chocolate

Toffees

Bubble gum

4 voted for Lollypops   ♟ ♟ ♟ ♟

7 voted for Ice cream   ♟ ♟ ♟ ♟ ♟ ♟ ♟·

6 voted for Chocolate   ♟ ♟ ♟ ♟ ♟ ♟

5 voted for Toffees   ♟ ♟ ♟ ♟ ♟

3 voted for Bubble gum ♟ ♟ ♟

Complete the pictogram then answer the questions.

1. How many pupils voted for bubble gum?

2. How many pupils voted for ice cream?

3. How many pupils voted for toffees?

4. How many pupils voted for chocolate?

5. Which item got most votes?

6. Which item got least votes?

7. Which item got 6 votes?

8. Which item got 4 votes?

9. Which item got 5 votes?

10. How many votes were cast in all?

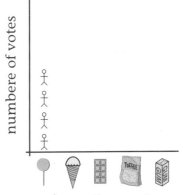

numbere of votes

favourite sweets

Exercise 10

If you asked the whole school to vote for their favourite sweet, the pictogram would be very big and hard to understand. You need a scale.
In this pictogram one figure (⚻) shows each 10 votes.

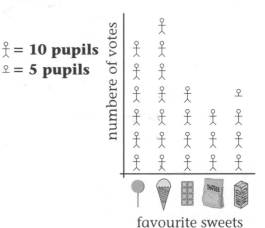

⚻ = **10 pupils**
⚲ = **5 pupils**

1. How many pupils voted for lollypops?
2. How many pupils voted for ice cream?
3. How many pupils voted for chocolate?
4. How many pupils voted for toffees?
5. How many pupils voted for bubble gum?

Remember each figure (⚻) = 10 votes.

DRAWING A PICTOGRAM

To draw a pictogram:
a Draw two **axes**. Measure out the axes carefully.
b Label the columns neatly:
  'Bus' 'Walk' 'Cycle' etc.
c Label the axes.
d Draw in the figures: (e.g. ⚲).

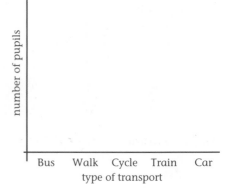

Exercise 11

Here is a tally chart of how pupils make their way to school.

Type of transport	Tally	Frequency (total)
Bus	|||| |||| |||| |||| |||| |||| |||| ||||	
Walk	|||| |||| |||| |||| |||| |||| |||| |||| |||| |||| |||| ||||	
Cycle	|||| |||| |||| |||| |||| ||||	
Train	|||| ||||	
Car	|||| |||| |||| ||||	

Make a pictogram of this information. Use each figure (⚻) to show **10 pupils**.

Exercise 12

Here is a tally chart of pupils attending a Youth Club.

Make a pictogram of this information.

Use each figure (♀) to show 10 pupils.

Use half the figure (♀) to show 5 pupils.

Day	Tally	Frequency (total)
Monday	卌 卌 卌 卌	
Tuesday	卌 卌 卌 卌 卌 卌	
Wednesday	卌 卌 卌 卌 卌 卌	
Thursday	卌 卌 卌 卌	
Friday	卌 卌 卌	

BAR CHARTS

Because pictograms take a long time to draw, a bar chart can be used.
Here is the same information displayed on a pictogram and a bar chart.

pictogram

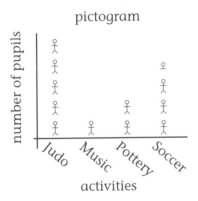

♀ = 10 pupils
♀ = 5 pupils

bar chart

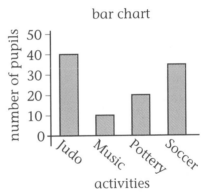

The two grids are **exactly the same**.
The bar chart uses bars instead of pictures.

Exercise 13

Re-draw these pictograms as bar charts.

1.

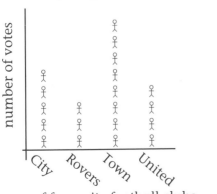

Survey of favourite football clubs
♀ = **1 pupil**

2.

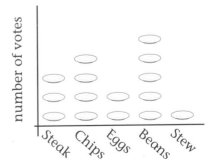

Survey of favourite foods. ⬭ = **5 portions**

THE MODE

Here is a bar chart showing the results
of a survey about favourite football teams.

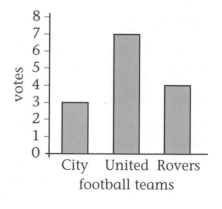

When you look at the bar chart you can see
that 'United' get the greatest number of votes.

The biggest group in a display is called the **mode**.

So, 'United' is **the mode**.

Exercise 14

What is the **mode** in each display?

1. Display of votes for
   class monitor.

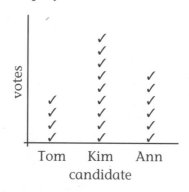

2. What people prefer to
   do on a night out.

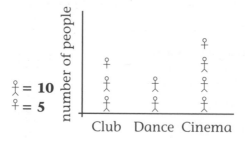

3. Favourite type of travel.

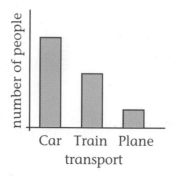

STATISTICS AT WORK

Exercise 15

Six children take part in a competition.
You can see their positions for each event in the four boxes.

Points		Darts		Cards		Chess		Table tennis	
1st = 11 points		1st	Mary	1st	Errol	1st	Tony	1st	Ann
2nd = 9 points		2nd	Tony	2nd	Mary	2nd	Ali	2nd	Tony
3rd = 7 points		3rd	Errol	3rd	Ann	3rd	Errol	3rd	Mary
4th = 5 points		4th	Ann	4th	Ali	4th	Mary	4th	Errol
5th = 3 points		5th	Ali	5th	Fred	5th	Ann	5th	Ali
6th = 1 point		6th	Fred	6th	Tony	6th	Fred	6th	Fred

1. Copy and complete this table.

Name	Points	Frequency (total)	Position
Ali	3 + 5 + 9 + 3	20	
Ann			
Errol			
Fred			
Mary			
Tony			

2. Complete the bar chart.

3. Which position did Ali come in chess?

4. Who came 4th in darts?

5. Who scored a total of 6 points?

6. Who came 6th in cards?

7. Who came 1st in table tennis?

8. Who came 5th in chess?

9. Which position did Ann come in darts?

10. What total score did Errol get?

11. How many points did Tony score in the cards contest?

12. Who scored 5 points in the darts contest?

13. What score was the mode?

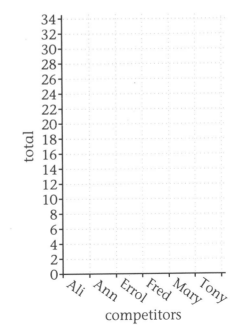

ε wɜivɜ яREVIEW 3

A. MEASUREMENT

Measure the height of these chess pieces.

1.

Pawn

2.

Rook

3.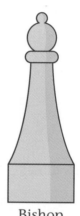

Bishop

4.

King

B. DRAWING

a Draw these shapes accurately.
b What is the perimeter of each shape?

1.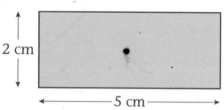

2 cm

5 cm

2.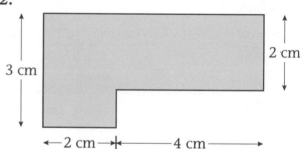

3 cm

2 cm

2 cm   4 cm

C. GREATER THAN/LESS THAN

> means greater than   < means less than

Copy out these problems and put in the correct sign.

1. 2 ☐ 4

2. 5 ☐ 6

3. 9 ☐ 5

4. 9 ☐ 8

5. 2 + 3 ☐ 8

6. 9 + 4 ☐ 12

7. 6 + 7 ☐ 14

8. 8 + 9 ☐ 19

9. 8 − 7 ☐ 3

10. 12 − 5 ☐ 9

11. 14 − 7 ☐ 8

12. 21 − 10 ☐ 9

D. ALGEBRA

Copy these out and fill in the missing numbers.

1. 6 + ☐ = 8

2. 8 + ☐ = 10

3. 6 + ☐ = 10

4. ☐ + 7 = 11

5. ☐ + 9 = 13

6. ☐ + 8 = 17

7. 9 − ☐ = 4

8. 12 − ☐ = 9

9. 18 − ☐ = 12

10. ☐ − 5 = 3

11. ☐ − 2 = 5

12. ☐ − 8 = 9

E. PERIMETER

Calculate the length of these perimeters. *These drawings are not full size.*
Remember: the perimeter of a shape is the distance once around the edge.

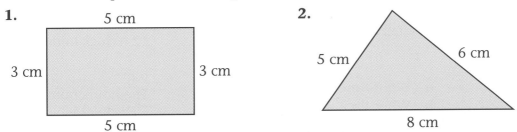

1. 5 cm, 3 cm, 3 cm, 5 cm

2. 5 cm, 6 cm, 8 cm

3.

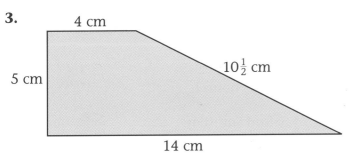

4 cm, $10\frac{1}{2}$ cm, 5 cm, 14 cm

F. ANGLES

Name these angles. Choose from: obtuse, reflex, acute, straight.

1. 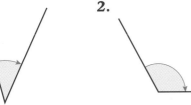 **2.** 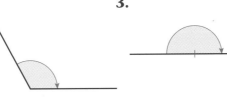 **3.** 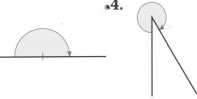 **4.**

5. Copy and complete these sentences.
  a A right angle is ____°.
  b Acute angles are more than ____° and less than ____°.
  c Obtuse angles are more than ____° and less than ____°
  d Reflex angles are more than ____° and less than ____°.
  e A straight line is an angle of ____°.

G. PATTERNS

See if you can draw this pattern in your book.
Use colour or shading.

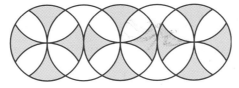

H. TIME

1. 3 p.m.

   a What time will it be in 2 hours?
   b What time will it be in 6 hours?
   c What time will it be in 8 hours?

> a.m.
> The hours from 12 o'clock midnight to 12 o'clock midday.
>
> p.m.
> The hours from 12 o'clock midday to 12 o'clock midnight.

2. 8 a.m.

   a What time will it be in $2\frac{1}{2}$ hours?
   b What time will it be in 3 hours?
   c What time will it be in $3\frac{1}{2}$ hours?

3. 1.30 p.m.

   a What time will it be in 6 hours?
   b What time will it be in $2\frac{1}{2}$ hours?
   c What time will it be in $4\frac{1}{2}$ hours?

4. _____ comes between Thursday and Saturday.

5. _____ comes between Sunday and Tuesday.

6. _____ comes after Saturday.

7. _____ comes after Tuesday.

8. _____ comes after Friday.

I. MONEY

| Tennis racket | Soccer ball | Track suit | Rugby boots |
| £40.50 | £15.50 | £45.25 | £32.00 |

1. If you bought the rugby boots, how much change would you get from £40?
2. If you bought the soccer ball, how much change would you get from £20?
3. How much would the tennis racket and the rugby boots cost altogether?
4. How much would the track suit and the soccer ball cost altogether?
5. How much would the track suit and the tennis racket cost altogether?
6. If the cost of the track suit was reduced by £4, how much would it cost?
7. If the rugby boots were reduced by £2.50, how much would they cost?
8. How much would two track suits cost?

J. NUMBER WORK

Write out the answers.

1. $4 + 5 + 3 = \square$ 2. $5 + 6 + 2 = \square$ 3. $8 + 6 + 7 = \square$

4. $9 + 6 + 5 = \square$ 5. $12 + 3 + 4 = \square$ 6. $15 + 8 + 5 = \square$

7. $\begin{array}{r} 12 \\ 14 \\ +\ \ 3 \\ \hline \end{array}$ 8. $\begin{array}{r} 20 \\ 6 \\ +\ 13 \\ \hline \end{array}$ 9. $\begin{array}{r} 23 \\ 17 \\ +\ \ 8 \\ \hline \end{array}$

10. $13 - 8 = \square$ 11. $24 - 7 = \square$ 12. $31 - 16 = \square$

13. $30 - 19 = \square$ 14. $42 - 26 = \square$ 15. $51 - 37 = \square$

16. $\begin{array}{r} 40 \\ -\ 19 \\ \hline \end{array}$ 17. $\begin{array}{r} 46 \\ -\ 37 \\ \hline \end{array}$ 18. $\begin{array}{r} 51 \\ -\ 23 \\ \hline \end{array}$

19. $4 \times 5 = \square$ 20. $5 \times 6 = \square$ 21. $7 \times 3 = \square$

22. $9 \div 3 = \square$ 23. $12 \div 2 = \square$ 24. $25 \div 5 = \square$

K. DECIMALS

1. Which of the drawings below show 0.1 coloured?

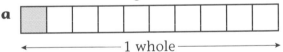

a

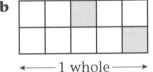

b

c

d

2. Which of these numbers is the same as two units and seven tenths?
   a 3.6   **b** 1.9   **c** 2.7   **d** 7.2

3. Which of these numbers is bigger than 6.4?
   a 5.9   **b** 6.8   **c** 0.9   **d** 6.3

4. Which of these numbers is smaller than 0.6?
   a 0.3   **b** 0.7   **c** 1.0   **d** 8.7

5. Which of these numbers shows 5 tenths?
   a 1.4   **b** 2.7   **c** 5.4   **d** 0.5

6. Copy these expressions. Use the > or the < sign to make the expressions true.
   a 6.1 ___ 6.0   **b** 0.9 ___ 1.0   **c** 0.5 ___ 0.1   **d** 7.0 ___ 0.7
   e 3.3 ___ 7.2   **f** 4.4 ___ 0.4   **g** 4.0 ___ 0.4   **h** 0.7 ___ 7.0

7. If a ruler is 10 cm long, one tenth of the length of the ruler will be ___ cm.

L. TIME

1. Copy the table below. Use the calendar on page 93 to help to fill in the table.

Month with 28 days	Months with 30 days	Months with 31 days

M. BASE TEN

1. What numbers are shown here?

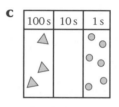

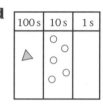

2. **a** In 125, what figure is shown in the tens column?
   b In 416, what figure is shown in the units column?
   c In 264, what figure is shown in the tens column?
   d In 359, what figure is shown in the hundreds column?
   e In 247, what figure is shown in the units column?
   f In 420, what figure is shown in the hundreds column?

3. Write out these numbers in figures
   a Two hundred and twenty-six.
   b Six hundred and sixty-five.
   c One hundred and fifty-one.
   d Four hundred and seventy.
   e Eight hundred and five.

N. FRACTIONS

1. Find one half ($\frac{1}{2}$) of each amount.

a    **b**    **c**

   d Find one half of 12   **e** Find one half of 20

2. Find one quarter ($\frac{1}{4}$) of each amount.

a    **b**    **c**

P. HANDLING DATA

1. Here is a drawing of Robert Wadlow, the world's tallest man.
The bar chart tells you how tall he was during his younger years.

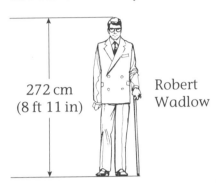

272 cm
(8 ft 11 in)

Robert
Wadlow

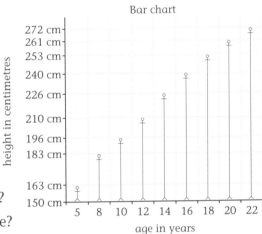

Bar chart

a How tall was Wadlow at 8 years of age?

b How tall was Wadlow at 14 years of age?

c How tall was Wadlow at 10 years of age?

d How tall was Wadlow at 18 years of age?

e How tall was Wadlow at 20 years of age?

f How old was he when his height was 210 cm?

g How old was he when his height was 240 cm?

h How old was he when his height was 163 cm?

2. a Record these dice scores on a tally chart and on a bar chart.

4	—	5	—	1	—	3	—	1	—	6	—	4	—	3	—	1	—	5	—	6
4	—	1	—	2	—	5	—	3	—	6	—	4	—	4	—	4	—	2	—	5
1	—	4	—	5	—	2	—	1	—	3	—	6	—	1	—	5	—	4	—	4

Number	Tally	Frequency (total)
1		
2		
3		
4		
5		
6		

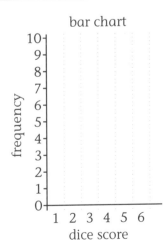

bar chart

b What is the mode?

17 STREET MATHS

TARGETS

Exercise 1

Here are the targets from a target shooting competition.
Each person had 5 shots.

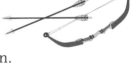

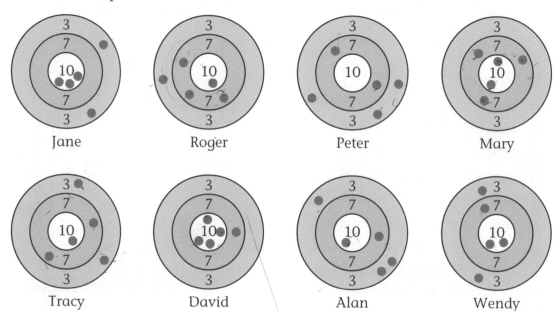

Jane   Roger   Peter   Mary

Tracy   David   Alan   Wendy

1. Copy and complete the table.

2. Who scored 23 points?

3. Who came second?

4. How many points did Wendy score?

5. Who came sixth?

6. Who scored 36 points?

7. How many points did Alan score?

8. Who came first?

9. Who hit most tens on the target?

10. Who scored no tens on the target?

11. Who scored 34 points?

Name	Points	Position
Jane	3 + 3 + 10 + 10 + 10 = 36	

NUMERACY PINBALL WIZARD

Exercise 2

In each pinball game, ★ means a score.

1. Work out the score for each go.

2. What is the total score after four goes?

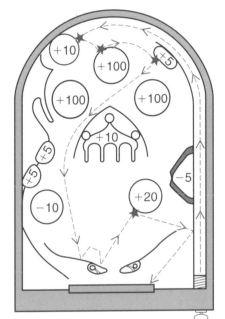

1st go

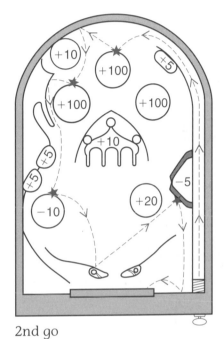

2nd go

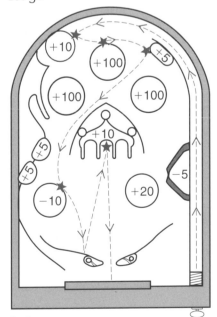

3rd go

4th go

 SPACE INVADER

Here is a space invader screen before the game starts.

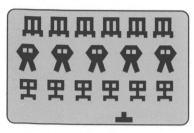

🎮 = 120 points

👾 = 50 points

👾 = 25 points

Exercise 3

Here are the final screens for these goes:

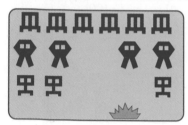 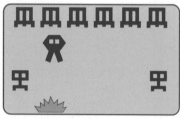 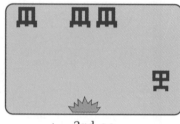

1st go   2nd go   3rd go

1. How much was scored on the first go?

2. How much was scored on the second go?

3. How much was scored on the third go?

4. What was the total score?

Exercise 4

Here are another three goes:

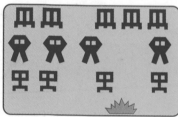  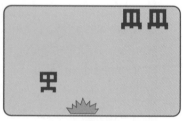

1st go   2nd go   3rd go

1. How much was scored on the first go?

2. How much was scored on the second go?

3. How much was scored on the third go?

4. What was the total score?